"Jennifer is changing the dinner game with this new cookbook for busy weeknights. Her recipes are healthy, approachable, and creative. I literally want to make everything from this cookbook!"

—GINA HOMOLKA, author of
The Skinnytaste Cookbook

"In *Once Upon a Chef: Weeknight/Weekend*, Jenn answers the question we've all asked a million times: What should I make for dinner? Whether you want a fast, flavorful, and family-friendly dish for a weeknight or a leisurely cooking project for a weekend, Jenn has you more than covered. With all these gorgeous recipes, you won't know what to make first!"

—JEANINE DONOFRIO, author of
Love and Lemons Every Day

"Jenn Segal's stellar new cookbook shines a bright spotlight on that perfect balance between delicious weeknight meals and the recipes that give us the best-ever weekend vibes. The recipes are as inventive as they are approachable!

—JUSTIN CHAPPLE, culinary
director-at-large, *Food & Wine*
and author of *Just Cook It!*

"Jennifer really knows how to write a cookbook that will have you saying 'yep, need to make that' to every single recipe. Her approachable demeanor, expert tips, and unfussy ingredients are exactly what you need to get delicious, foolproof meals on the table fast."

—LISA BRYAN
from Downshiftology

"*Once Upon a Chef* is full of luscious, sure-fire family favorites. I can't stop thinking about Lasagna Soup; Flat Iron Carne Asada; Arugula, Crispy Feta & Watermelon Salad; and French Apple Cake (plus a whole section full of meatballs that are sure to please even the pickiest families). Jennifer's recipes are welcoming, vibrant, and most important, doable! Organizing recipes by weekend and weeknight fare helps even the busiest parents approach the family table as the grounding, unifying force we all hope it can be."

—SARAH COPELAND,
author of *Instant Family Meals*

"Don't we all wish we could make restaurant-worthy meals for our families? Former chef Jennifer Segal gifts to us her drool-worthy dishes just as she does for her lucky family every night. *Once Upon a Chef: Weeknight/Weekend* is layered with meals you can cook and eat together, creating culinary memories in this magical inspired cookbook. You want to jump through the pages and devour everything, including Ginger Pork Sliders and Kids-Love-It Beefy Chili Mac! Home cooks, it's time to rejoice with your new go-to cookbook!"

—CATHERINE McCORD,
author of *Weelicious*

"Jennifer's new cookbook has much to offer—it's as though she is standing by your side in the kitchen talking you through the recipes like a dear friend. What's more, I always know her recipes will turn out delicious. They can be trusted and her clear, simple directions make them a pleasure to make."

—SYLVIA FOUNTAINE
from *Feasting at Home*

once upon a chef
WEEKNIGHT / WEEKEND

once upon a chef
WEEKNIGHT / WEEKEND

70 QUICK-FIX
WEEKNIGHT DINNERS

+

30 LUSCIOUS
WEEKEND RECIPES

Jennifer Segal

PHOTOGRAPHY BY
JOHNNY MILLER

Clarkson Potter Publishers
NEW YORK

Published by Clarkson Potter/Publishers,
an imprint of Random House, a division of
Penguin Random House LLC, New York.
clarksonpotter.com

CLARKSON POTTER is a trademark and
POTTER with colophon is a registered
trademark of Penguin Random House LLC.

Library of Congress Cataloging-in-Publication
Data

Names: Segal, Jennifer, author.
Title: Once upon a chef : weeknight/weekend:
70 quick-fix weeknight dinners + 30 luscious
weekend recipes / Jennifer Segal.
Description: First edition. | New York : Clarkson
Potter/Publishers, 2021. | Includes index. |
Identifiers: LCCN 2021015692 (print) |
LCCN 2021015693 (ebook) | ISBN
9780593231838 | ISBN 9780593231845 (ebook)
Subjects: LCSH: Cooking. | LCGFT: Cookbooks.
Classification: LCC TX714 .S444 2021 (print) |
LCC TX714 (ebook) | DDC
641.5--dc23
LC record available at https://lccn.loc.
gov/2021015692
LC ebook record available at https://lccn.loc.
gov/2021015693

Photographer: Johnny Miller
Food Stylist: Rebecca Jurkevich
Prop Stylist: Sarah Smart
Editor: Raquel Pelzel
Designer: Jan Derevjanik
Production Editor: Serena Wang
Production Manager: Kelli Tokos
Composition: Merri Ann Morrell
Copy Editor: Carole Berglie

ISBN 978-0-593-23183-8
Ebook ISBN 978-0-593-23184-5

Printed in China

10 9 8 7 6 5 4 3 2 1

First Edition

To my husband, Michael,
who makes me laugh,
and my kids, Zach and Anna,
who fill my heart.
Let's eat!

Contents

Introduction

One atypical evening last year, when I was in the thick of writing this cookbook and the country was in the beginning of a pandemic, my family was sitting around the kitchen table after dinner. The plates had all been cleared, but much to my surprise, Zach and Anna, my two teenagers, had not bolted upstairs to finish their homework or escape our nosy questions; rather, they were lingering at the table discussing their crazy new normal: missing their friends, kids dozing off during Zoom class, and how bored they were being stuck at home 24/7 with us. One conversation rolled seamlessly into the next, and soon we were talking about politics and world events. My husband, Michael, and I looked at each other in astonishment—here were two bright kids with their own thoughtful points of view, engaging in meaningful conversation at the dinner table. This was new!

In 2020, family dinner—and breakfast and lunch, for that matter—took on a whole new meaning. Life slowed to a crawl. All the kids' extracurriculars were erased from our schedule. Michael was working from home, literally in the next room. Suddenly my family was sitting together around the kitchen table several times a day. It was a ton of cooking, even for me, but the silver lining was having more time to cook and connect over family meals.

When I first started collecting recipes as a new mom, years before I started my website *Once Upon a Chef,* I kept them in a giant three-ring binder divided into two main sections: Weeknight and Weekend. That binder is long gone—it eventually became my blog—but to this day, it's how I think about cooking. Like most everyone else, I need lots of quick and delicious weeknight dinners, but I don't always want to rush around the kitchen—sometimes, I want to find joy in it.

With everyone suddenly working or "schooling" from home, I relied heavily on those easy weeknight recipes to get meals on the table without stress or fuss because, let's face it, we all have had enough of that in our lives already! On the flip side, with endless time at home and lots of nervous energy to expend, my leisurely weekend recipes served not only as a calming activity but also as a welcome source of comfort food.

I know I wasn't the only one experiencing the upside of cooking all of our meals. My sister-in-law, Sheryl, whose kids are 17, 21, and 23, told me that for the first time ever, her family was sitting down together for dinner every single night. My dear friend Dana assigned each of her kids dinner duty one night a week—everything from planning, to cooking, to cleaning up—not only to keep them occupied but also to teach them how to cook. My readers learned to bake their own artisan breads, planted herb gardens with their kids, and cooked dinner with faraway family over Zoom. Though difficult in so many ways, the time at home was a reminder that cooking and sharing food is one of the best ways to create wonderful memories and strong family bonds.

When I think back to my own childhood, the first image that pops into my mind is sitting around the kitchen island eating dinner, listening to my parents share stories about work. My mom didn't love to cook, to say the least—she jokes now that she would have made UberEats an instant success, had it been around in the seventies—but she made family dinner a priority, and what she cooked, she cooked well. One of my most treasured possessions is her old green tin recipe box, filled with splattered index cards written in her distinctive cursive, and faded magazine clippings that tell the story of my childhood and show how much she cared.

This cookbook is filled with recipes that make up my family's memories. It's the food I make on weeknights and weekends, birthdays and holidays, crazy days and lazy days. It's old family favorites that fill the house with familiar aromas and warmth—and new recipes, too, because kids grow up, palates change, and we all get tired of the same ol' same.

It's the Strawberries & Cream Layer Cake (page 252) that I make every year for my husband's June birthday, the Eastern Shore Crab Soup (page 25) we discovered on the Chesapeake Bay, and the "Lucky" Sausage & Cheddar Drop Biscuits (page 216) I bake on the mornings my kids have to fuel up for a big test or game.

It's the Baked Ziti with Sausage (page 104) I make on Friday nights when my parents come over because it's my dad's favorite. It's loads of just-plain-delicious and kid-friendly weeknight dinners that have earned a spot in our rotation, like Saucy Sesame-Ginger Meatballs (page 119) and Pecorino & Rosemary-Crusted Chicken (page 131). And, finally, it's "cheffy" recipes, like Dijon & Panko-Crusted Rack of Lamb (page 167) or Arugula, Crispy Feta & Watermelon Salad with Balsamic Vinaigrette (page 37), because sometimes there are good things to celebrate and the chef in me needs to eat, too.

My hope is that the recipes in this book bring the people you care about around the table, and that they help you find joy in cooking, too. At the end of the day, sometimes we cook because we have to and sometimes because we love to, but either way, the reward is the same. My motivation during the week centers on my family getting the nourishment and face-to-face time we all need—and I love how busy nights prove our ability to get through the storm and anchor ourselves at the table. On the weekends, I find comfort digging my hands into pillowy dough or tending a

slow-cooking stew that fills the house with delicious anticipation, and I feel a sense of satisfaction when I've created something delicious that can be shared with family or friends.

Finally, since cooking is more fun when recipes turn out as promised, know that I have thoroughly tested every recipe in this book in my home kitchen. I'm also lucky enough to have hundreds of volunteer recipe testers—avid home cooks, retired home economics teachers, and even some aspiring teenage chefs—who helped me ensure that the recipes are foolproof and family-approved. I hope that with each recipe completed, you feel more confident in the kitchen. And remember, I'm just an email or DM (if you're an Instagram or Facebook person!) away if you ever have any questions. Drop me a line through my website—I'd love to hear from you!

xo Jenn

Weeknights

The first question my kids usually ask when they walk in the door is, "What's for dinner?"

Much as I love to cook, I don't harbor any romantic notions about weeknight cooking. Whether you work outside the home or from home, or care for kids all day long, cooking dinner during the week can often feel like a chore—and this is true even for a professional like me. However, I find that once I wrap my head around *what* I'm cooking for dinner, pull out my ingredients, and turn on some music, weeknight cooking is doable—enjoyable, even. Most important, when we're all sitting around the table talking about our day, and everyone goes for seconds, I feel a true sense of pride and contentment. My husband jokes that I enjoy compliments more than the average gal, but "Mom, this is so good" is music to my ears. A good homemade dinner puts a happy exclamation point on the day.

The challenge with weeknight recipes is that, oftentimes, what we gain in time and convenience we lose in flavor. In these chapters, I'll show you how to create flavorful, restaurant-quality meals, even on a busy schedule. The recipes reflect my way of thinking that dinner does not always have to be a protein, a vegetable, and a starch. Sometimes it's a hearty soup with a crusty wedge of fresh bread, a vibrant salad, a hot baked sandwich, or even breakfast food (if you've never had sausage and egg burritos for dinner, you're missing out!).

So, what makes a recipe a weeknight recipe? In general, for me, it should require no more than 45 minutes active prep/cooking time. Some recipes are naturally quick, like Chorizo-Style Burgers with Spiced Ketchup (page 82) or Ciabatta Pesto Pizza (page 85). And funny enough, the fanciest-sounding recipes are often the fastest; you can whip up Pan-Seared Filet Mignon with Red Wine Sauce (page 164) between soccer practice and bedtime—I promise (I've done it).

Other weeknight recipes require a little forethought—time to brine or marinate—but once that's done, they come together in a flash. You'll see a "heads up" note at the top of each of those, so you don't get started at 7 P.M. and then realize dinner won't be ready until midnight. When I'm making these kinds of recipes, I'll often start them the night before when I'm cleaning up after dinner or in the morning before the kids wake up.

Some of my favorite weeknight dishes are quick on the front end but require a longer stretch in the oven. Sheet Pan Roast Chicken with Artichokes, Potatoes, Carrots & Peas (page 127), for example, takes 15 minutes to prep, then bakes unattended in the oven for almost an hour—the perfect length of time to clean up the kitchen, pour yourself a glass of wine, and change into your comfy clothes before the timer dings.

Finally, there's dessert, because even weeknight dinners deserve sweet endings: Brownie Pudding (page 176), Malted Milkshakes (page 183), French Apple Cake (page 184), and more family-friendly sweets you can make on the fly. The desserts in this chapter are made from ingredients you can always keep on hand and are simple enough even for kids to make (I had several teenagers test the recipes!). Whether you're having people for dinner, celebrating a happy occasion, or just in the mood for a treat, these low-effort–big-reward desserts will end your day on a sweet note.

Soup for Supper

Southwestern Corn Chowder 18

Coconut Curry Chicken & Rice Noodle Soup 21

Smoky Chickpea, Red Lentil & Vegetable Soup 22

Eastern Shore Crab Soup 25

Pumpkin Leek Soup 26

Creamy Potato Soup with Bacon, Cheddar & Chives 29

Lasagna Soup with Ricotta Cream 30

Southwestern Corn Chowder

MAKE-AHEAD
INSTRUCTIONS

Before adding the sour cream, scallions, and cilantro, the soup can be made up to 2 days ahead and refrigerated. Reheat on the stovetop over medium heat, and proceed with the recipe.

PRO TIP

To scrape the kernels from the cobs, place the corn on a clean dish towel set over a cutting board, then use a sharp knife to cut the kernels off the cobs. (The dish towel prevents the kernels from bouncing all over the place.) Alternatively, you can invert a small bowl inside a larger bowl. Hold the cob upright, flat end down, on top of the inverted bowl and use a sharp knife to slice downward as close to the cob as possible.

I think of this chowder as a summer-into-fall soup, perfect for when the nights turn cooler and you're looking for new and interesting ways to use up the last corn of the season. It's filling on its own, but if you'd like to bulk it up, crispy bacon, shredded chicken (a rotisserie chicken from the supermarket works great), grilled shrimp, or fresh lump crabmeat would all be delicious additions. And you can never go wrong with chips and guac on the side.

I like this soup a bit spicy, so I mince about half the jalapeño seeds and ribs and toss them in with the onion and pepper. If you'd like more control over the heat, you can add cayenne pepper at the end or offer hot sauce at the table.

Serves 4

4 tablespoons (½ stick/2 ounces/ 56 g) unsalted butter

1 medium yellow onion, diced

1 red bell pepper, diced

1 medium jalapeño pepper, seeded and finely diced (save the seeds and ribs; see headnote)

¼ cup (33 g) all-purpose flour

2 cups (480 mL) chicken broth

2 cups (480 mL) whole milk

2 teaspoons salt

2 teaspoons ground cumin

½ teaspoon ground coriander

1 pound (454 g) baby potatoes (yellow, red, or purple), cut into ½-inch (13 mm) pieces

3 cups (480 g) fresh corn kernels, scraped from 5 cobs (see Pro Tip)

⅓ cup (80 g) sour cream

3 scallions (dark green parts only), thinly sliced

3 tablespoons chopped fresh cilantro (optional)

1 lime, cut into wedges, for serving

1. Melt the butter in a large saucepan or Dutch oven over medium-high heat. Add the onion, bell pepper, and jalapeño and cook, stirring frequently, until softened, 5 to 7 minutes. Do not brown. Add the flour and cook, stirring constantly, for 1 minute.

2. Add the broth, 1 cup (240 mL) of the milk, and the salt, cumin, coriander, and potatoes; bring to a boil. The soup will seem thick; that's okay. Reduce the heat to low, cover the pan, and simmer, stirring once halfway through so that the potatoes don't stick to the bottom of the pan, until the potatoes are tender, 12 to 15 minutes (if your potatoes are not tender at this point, just continue simmering until they are).

3. Meanwhile, in a blender, puree the remaining 1 cup (240 mL) of milk with 1 cup (160 g) of the corn until smooth.

4. Add the corn puree to the soup along with the remaining 2 cups (320 g) corn; bring to a simmer. Off the heat, stir in the sour cream, scallions, and cilantro (if using). Taste and adjust seasoning if necessary. Ladle the soup into bowls and serve with lime wedges.

Coconut Curry Chicken & Rice Noodle Soup

This spicy, fragrant, slurpy noodle soup, inspired by some of my favorite Thai restaurant dishes, is like sunshine on a dreary day. What's more, it's made with rotisserie chicken and Thai pantry staples (available in most supermarkets)— such as green curry paste, fish sauce, coconut milk, and fresh ginger—so it's almost instant gratification. Whether I'm feeling worn down or just in need of a little comfort, there is nothing like a bowl of chicken noodle soup, and this is one of my favorite renditions. Be sure to keep the rice noodles separate from the soup until ready to serve. If you put them in the broth before serving, they will continue to cook and become too soft.

MAKE-AHEAD INSTRUCTIONS

Before adding the rice noodles, chicken, and garnishes, the soup can be made up to 2 days ahead and refrigerated. Reheat on the stovetop over medium heat, and proceed with the recipe.

SOURCING SAVVY

Fish sauce is a salty, savory condiment made from anchovies, salt, and water that's often used in East Asian cooking. It adds a rich umami flavor to sauces, marinades, and salad dressings. You can find it in most supermarkets.

Serves 4

1 tablespoon vegetable oil

½ cup (60 g) thinly sliced shallot (from 1 large shallot)

1 tablespoon minced fresh ginger (from a 1-inch/2.5 cm knob)

2 tablespoons Thai green curry paste

4 cups (960 mL) low-sodium chicken broth

1 (13.5-ounce/400 mL) can coconut milk

2 tablespoons fish sauce

4 teaspoons packed dark brown sugar

2 tablespoons fresh lime juice (from 1 lime)

½ teaspoon ground turmeric

FOR SERVING

4 ounces (113 g) thin rice noodles

2 cups (260 g) cooked shredded chicken (from a rotisserie chicken)

3 tablespoons chopped fresh cilantro

3 scallions (light and dark green parts), thinly sliced

Sriracha sauce

Lime wedges

1. Heat the oil in a large saucepan or Dutch oven over medium-low heat. Add the shallot and ginger and cook, stirring frequently, until softened, 3 to 5 minutes. Add the curry paste and cook, stirring constantly, for 1 minute more. Add the chicken broth, coconut milk, fish sauce, brown sugar, lime juice, and turmeric; bring to a gentle simmer. Continue simmering, uncovered, for 5 minutes.

2. Meanwhile, cook the rice noodles according to the package instructions.

3. When ready to serve, taste the soup and adjust the seasoning if necessary. Gently reheat the noodles in the microwave if necessary. Divide the noodles and chicken among serving bowls.

4. Ladle the soup over the top and sprinkle with cilantro and scallions. Serve with sriracha and lime wedges.

Smoky Chickpea, Red Lentil & Vegetable Soup

MAKE-AHEAD/FREEZER-FRIENDLY INSTRUCTIONS

The soup can be made up to 3 days ahead and refrigerated, or frozen for up to 3 months. Defrost it overnight in the refrigerator and then reheat it on the stovetop over medium heat.

SOURCING SAVVY

It's important to use red lentils, as opposed to another variety; they cook quickly and thicken the soup nicely. The recipe only calls for ⅓ cup; don't be tempted to add more or the soup will become too thick.

For a vegetarian recipe made almost entirely from pantry staples (and I mean true staples, not staples from some well-stocked dream kitchen), this soup is surprisingly delicious. It's thickened by pureeing a portion of the soup and then stirring it back into the pot. The soup takes just 30 minutes to come together, start to finish, yet tastes like you spent all day in the kitchen, and it's good for you, too. For the cooked vegetables, feel free to use any quick-cooking, frozen, or leftover vegetables you have on hand. The recipe is extremely flexible and very hearty!

Serves 4 to 6

2 tablespoons olive oil

1 medium yellow onion, finely chopped

4 garlic cloves, minced

1 large carrot, diced

Heaping ¼ teaspoon smoked paprika

¾ teaspoon ground cumin

4 cups (960 mL) low-sodium vegetable or chicken broth

1 (14.5-ounce/411 g) can diced tomatoes, with their juice

⅓ cup (60 g) red lentils

½ teaspoon dried thyme

2 bay leaves

1 teaspoon salt

¼ teaspoon freshly ground black pepper

1 (15.5-ounce/439 g) can chickpeas, drained and rinsed

1 cup (120 g) cooked vegetables, such as peas or chopped green beans

1. Heat the oil in a large saucepan or Dutch oven over medium heat. Add the onion and cook, stirring occasionally, until soft, about 5 minutes. Add the garlic, carrot, smoked paprika, and cumin; cook, stirring frequently so the garlic doesn't brown, about 2 minutes more.

2. Add the broth, diced tomatoes, lentils, thyme, bay leaves, salt, and pepper and bring to a boil. Cover the pot and reduce the heat to a simmer; cook for 10 minutes. Add the chickpeas, re-cover the pot, and cook 10 minutes more. Fish out the bay leaves.

3. Transfer 2 cups (480 mL) of the soup to a blender and puree until smooth, (Be sure to remove the center knob from the blender lid and cover the lid with a dish towel to avoid splatters.) Add the pureed soup back to the pot and stir. Taste and adjust the seasoning if necessary; if you want the soup to be thicker, puree a bit more of the soup.

4. Add the cooked vegetables to the soup and simmer until the soup is hot and the vegetables are warmed through. Ladle the soup into bowls and serve.

Eastern Shore Crab Soup

Filled with fresh lump crabmeat and seasoned with Old Bay, a spice blend that comes from my home state of Maryland, this soup tastes like a day on the Eastern Shore. In fact, the recipe was scribbled down on a piece of paper for me by the chef from the Hyatt Regency Chesapeake Bay, when we were there celebrating my parents' 50th wedding anniversary. It is unapologetically rich and indulgent. Please don't be tempted to substitute the half-and-half with milk. It won't thicken properly unless you add more butter and flour, which would defeat the whole purpose of making it lighter by using milk instead of half-and-half. I promise, it's 100 percent worth it!

Serves 4

3 tablespoons unsalted butter

3 tablespoons all-purpose flour

4 cups (960 mL) half-and-half

1 teaspoon Dijon mustard

1 tablespoon Old Bay seasoning, plus more for serving

¼ teaspoon salt

⅛ teaspoon freshly ground black pepper

2 tablespoons dry sherry

½ pound (227 g) lump crabmeat, picked over to remove any shells

Finely chopped chives, for garnish

Lemon wedges, for serving (optional)

1. Melt the butter in a large saucepan or Dutch oven over medium-low heat. Add the flour and whisk for about 1 minute, until well blended.

2. Whisking constantly, gradually add the half-and-half to the pot. Add the mustard, Old Bay, salt, and pepper. Bring to a boil, whisking frequently (be sure to scrape the edges of the pot, where the flour mixture tends to settle). As soon as the soup starts to boil, reduce the heat to a simmer and cook, uncovered, until thickened, about 30 seconds.

3. Stir in the sherry and crabmeat. Taste and adjust seasoning if necessary. If the soup is too thick, add water, little by little, to thin it out (it will thicken the longer it sits on the stove, even off of the heat). Ladle the soup into bowls and sprinkle with the chives. Serve with lemon wedges, if desired.

MAKE-AHEAD INSTRUCTIONS

The soup can be made (up until the point of adding the sherry and crabmeat) up to 2 days ahead and refrigerated. It will thicken up in the refrigerator, so thin it with a little water when reheating if necessary. Add the sherry and crabmeat right before serving.

SOURCING SAVVY

Look for unpasteurized crabmeat, which is sold in a clear plastic container usually resting on ice in the seafood department. If it's not available, the second-best option is refrigerated pasteurized crabmeat, such as Phillip's, which is readily available year-round. Avoid shelf-stable canned crabmeat, which contains additives that affect the taste and texture of the meat.

Old Bay seasoning is a zesty spice blend made from salt, celery seed, paprika, mustard, and pepper, to name just a few of the ingredients, that you can find near the seafood department at most supermarkets.

Pumpkin Leek Soup

When we think of pumpkin, we usually think of autumn sweets, like pumpkin pie and pumpkin bread, but pumpkin's earthy flavor is wonderful in savory dishes, too. This velvety soup is flavored with leeks, apples, and maple syrup, so it has those sweet undertones that you expect in a squash soup, but also with smoky cumin and spicy cayenne pepper to balance out the flavor. If that sounds like an unusual combination, have faith—one reader wrote to me that it was one of the best soups she's made in fifty-three years of marriage! I know canned pumpkin feels like cheating, but it's a great shortcut; if you'd like to roast and puree fresh pumpkin, you'll need 1¾ cups.

Serves 4 to 6

4 tablespoons (½ stick/2 ounces/ 56 g) unsalted butter

2½ pounds (1.1 kg) leeks (white and light green parts only), washed well and thinly sliced (see Pro Tip)

4 garlic cloves, roughly chopped

1 (15-ounce/425 g) can pumpkin puree, preferably Libby's

1 apple, peeled, cored, and roughly chopped

6 cups (1.4 L) low-sodium chicken broth

5 tablespoons (80 mL) maple syrup

1½ teaspoons salt

½ teaspoon ground cumin

⅛ to ¼ teaspoon cayenne pepper

1½ teaspoons chopped fresh thyme, plus leaves for garnish

1½ teaspoons chopped fresh sage

¼ cup (60 mL) heavy cream, plus more for garnish

1. Melt the butter in a large saucepan or Dutch oven over medium heat. Add the leeks and garlic and cook, stirring occasionally, until softened, about 10 minutes.

2. Add the pumpkin puree, apple, broth, maple syrup, salt, cumin, cayenne, thyme, and sage. Bring to a boil, then reduce the heat to low and simmer, uncovered, for 20 minutes.

3. Add the cream. Use an immersion blender to puree the soup until completely smooth. (Alternatively, cool the soup slightly and use a blender to puree it in batches. Be sure to remove the center knob from the blender and cover the lid with a dish towel to avoid splatters.) Ladle the soup into bowls and garnish with a swirl of cream (see Pro Tip) and fresh thyme leaves, if desired.

Creamy Potato Soup

WITH BACON, CHEDDAR & CHIVES

This soup is so hearty and comforting that it practically wraps you up in a big hug. My kids think the addition of butter, sour cream, and bacon makes it taste like a loaded baked potato in soup form. Pair it with a light salad and dinner is done!

Serves 6 to 8

6 slices (8 ounces/227 g) thick-cut bacon, cut into ½-inch (13 mm) pieces

1 large yellow onion, roughly chopped

4 large garlic cloves, smashed and peeled (see Pro Tip)

2 tablespoons all-purpose flour

6 cups (1.4 L) chicken broth

3 pounds (1.4 kg) russet potatoes, peeled and cut into 1-inch (2.5 cm) cubes

1½ teaspoons salt

½ teaspoon freshly ground black pepper

½ teaspoon dried thyme

1 cup (240 g) sour cream

3 tablespoons unsalted butter

3 tablespoons chopped fresh chives

1 cup (4 ounces/120 g) shredded Cheddar cheese

1. In a large saucepan or Dutch oven over medium heat, cook the bacon, stirring frequently, until crisp, 8 to 10 minutes. Using a slotted spoon, transfer the bacon to a paper towel–lined plate and set aside. Pour off and discard all but about 2 tablespoons of the bacon fat.

2. Return the pot to the stove over medium heat. Add the onion and garlic and cook, stirring frequently, until the onion is soft and translucent, about 5 minutes. Do not brown; reduce the heat if necessary. Add the flour and stir until dissolved, about 30 seconds.

3. Pour in the chicken broth, stirring with a wooden spoon to scrape any browned bits off the bottom of the pan. Increase the heat to high and bring to a boil. Carefully add the potatoes, along with the salt, pepper, and thyme, and bring to a boil again. Reduce the heat to low, cover, and cook until the potatoes are very tender, 20 to 25 minutes.

4. Off the heat, use an immersion blender to puree the soup until completely smooth. (Alternatively, cool the soup slightly, then puree in a blender in batches. Be sure to remove the center knob in the lid, and cover it with a kitchen towel, to allow the steam to escape.) Add the sour cream and butter and whisk by hand until the butter is melted and the sour cream is incorporated. Taste and adjust the seasoning if necessary. Ladle the soup into bowls and top with the chives, cheese, and reserved bacon.

MAKE-AHEAD INSTRUCTIONS

The soup can be made up to 2 days ahead and refrigerated. (Hold off on adding the bacon, chives, and cheese until you serve the soup.) Keep in mind that it will thicken up quite a bit in the refrigerator. Reheat over medium heat until hot, and thin, if necessary, by whisking in a little water or milk.

PRO TIPS

To smash a garlic clove, put an unpeeled clove on your cutting board, lay your chef's knife on top of it, and hit the flat side of the knife blade firmly with the heel of your hand; this will smash the garlic clove underneath, and the peel will slip right off. (Since this soup gets pureed, you don't need to bother chopping the garlic. Leaving it in large pieces also prevents it from burning.)

To make bacon easier to work with, stick it in the freezer to firm up for 15 minutes before cutting.

Lasagna Soup WITH RICOTTA CREAM

MAKE-AHEAD INSTRUCTIONS

Before adding the cooked pasta and ricotta topping, the soup can be refrigerated for 2 days. Reheat on the stovetop over medium heat until simmering, add the pasta, and simmer until the pasta is cooked through.

Lasagna soup may sound gimmicky, but this really does taste like lasagna. The good news is that it's a whole lot easier to make. This isn't a soup in the traditional "light dinner" sense—it's almost as hearty as lasagna itself. I use reginetti noodles, which are like miniature ruffled lasagna noodles, but any short pasta shape will work; just avoid actual lasagna noodles, as they are a bit unwieldy to eat in soup. Serve with a warm baguette to soak up the broth.

Serves 4 to 6

6 ounces (170 g) short pasta, such as reginetti, shells, or macaroni (about 2 heaping cups)

2 tablespoons extra-virgin olive oil

1 pound (454 g) hot Italian sausage, removed from casings

4 garlic cloves, finely chopped

4 cups (960 mL) chicken broth

1 (28-ounce/794 g) can crushed tomatoes

1¼ teaspoons salt, plus a pinch

1 teaspoon sugar

½ teaspoon dried oregano

¼ teaspoon red pepper flakes

1 bay leaf

¾ cup (180 mL) heavy cream

½ cup (50 g) finely grated pecorino Romano cheese, plus more for serving

¼ cup (10 g) chopped fresh basil, plus more for serving

1 cup (240 g) whole-milk ricotta, at room temperature

1. Bring a medium pot of salted water to a boil. Cook the pasta to al dente according to the package instructions. Drain and set aside.

2. Meanwhile, heat the oil in a large saucepan or Dutch oven over medium-high heat. Add the sausage and cook, stirring frequently and breaking it up, until browned and just cooked through, 5 to 6 minutes. Transfer the sausage to a small colander set over a bowl, leaving the fat in the pan.

3. Reduce the heat to low, add the garlic to the pan, and cook, stirring constantly, until fragrant, about 30 seconds. Do not brown. Add the chicken broth, tomatoes, salt, sugar, oregano, red pepper flakes, and bay leaf and bring to a boil. Reduce the heat to medium-low and simmer vigorously, uncovered, for 10 minutes. Add the cream and cook for a few minutes more. Discard the bay leaf, then use a large spoon to skim off any excess grease. Add the reserved sausage, drained pasta, ¼ cup (25 g) of the pecorino Romano, and the basil to the pan. Stir to combine, then taste and adjust seasoning if necessary.

4. In a small bowl, stir the ricotta with the remaining ¼ cup (25 g) pecorino Romano and a generous pinch of salt.

5. Ladle the soup into serving bowls and top with a generous dollop of the ricotta mixture and more basil. Pass more grated pecorino Romano at the table.

Mighty Salads

Tabbouleh with Cedar Plank Salmon 34

Arugula, Crispy Feta & Watermelon Salad
with Balsamic Vinaigrette 37

Summer Garden Salad with Grilled Shrimp
& Fresh Herb Vinaigrette 39

Classic Cobb with Dijon Vinaigrette 43

Pan-Seared Steak, Baby Greens & Roasted
Beet Salad with Honey-Dijon Vinaigrette 45

Muffuletta Salad with Olive Vinaigrette 49

Soba Chicken Noodle Salad
with Ginger Peanut Dressing 50

Tabbouleh

WITH CEDAR PLANK SALMON

HEADS UP

Allow at least 1 hour for soaking the cedar plank. You'll also need at least 30 minutes to marinate the salmon, but you can do that while you prepare the bulgur and vegetables.

MAKE-AHEAD INSTRUCTIONS

The bulgur salad can be fully prepared and refrigerated up to a day ahead of time.

SOURCING SAVVY

Bulgur is a whole grain made from cracked wheat, commonly used in Middle Eastern and Mediterranean dishes, like tabbouleh. It has a nutty flavor and chewy texture. Since it is parboiled and dried before it is packaged, it cooks very quickly. It is sold in most large supermarkets and organic food stores (you can often find it in the bulk bins). This recipe calls for medium-grind bulgur, which is the most common (the grains are about the size of sesame seeds); coarse-grind bulgur is slightly coarser and may be substituted.

If there's one recipe in this book that epitomizes the way I love to eat, it's this one: bright Mediterranean flavors, nutritious yet satisfying ingredients, and not a lot of cleanup! Tabbouleh is a Middle Eastern salad made from quick-cooking bulgur, fresh herbs, and chopped vegetables. It would be good with grilled salmon alone, but marinating and grilling the salmon on a cedar plank adds layers of flavor—plus, you don't have to worry about the fish sticking to the grill. To save time, ask your fishmonger to remove the skin from the salmon. If you need to do it yourself, see page 146 for instructions.
• PHOTOGRAPH ON PAGE 32

Serves 4

1 or 2 cedar grilling planks, depending on size (see Pro Tip)

6 tablespoons (90 mL) extra-virgin olive oil

Salt and freshly ground black pepper

2 teaspoons grated lemon zest (from 2 lemons)

3 garlic cloves, minced

4 (6-ounce/170 g) salmon fillets, skin removed

1¼ cups (300 mL) water

1 cup (160 g) medium-grind bulgur wheat

2 tablespoons fresh lemon juice (from 1 lemon)

1 teaspoon ground cumin

1 teaspoon honey

1 small English/hothouse cucumber, halved, seeded, and finely diced

¾ cup (105 g) grape tomatoes, halved

⅓ cup (13 g) finely chopped fresh dill

⅓ cup (13 g) finely chopped fresh Italian parsley

⅓ cup (16 g) thinly sliced scallions (light and green parts; from 1 bunch)

1. Fill a large bowl or sink with water. Soak the cedar plank(s) for at least 1 hour.

2. In a baking dish large enough to hold the salmon, combine 3 tablespoons of the oil, a scant ½ teaspoon salt, ½ teaspoon pepper, the lemon zest, and two-thirds of the garlic. Place the salmon in the dish and turn to coat evenly; marinate in the refrigerator for at least 30 minutes and up to 4 hours.

3. In a small pot, bring the water and ½ teaspoon salt to a rapid boil. Add the bulgur, stir to moisten, then cover the pot and remove from the heat. Let sit for 25 to 30 minutes, until all the water is absorbed. Let the bulgur cool to room temperature.

4. In a large bowl, whisk together the remaining 3 tablespoons oil, ¾ teaspoon salt, ½ teaspoon pepper, the remaining third of the garlic, and the lemon juice, cumin, and honey. Add the bulgur, the cucumber, tomatoes, dill, parsley, and scallions. Toss well, then taste and adjust seasoning if necessary.

5. Preheat the grill to medium-high heat (about 450°F/235°C).

6. Pat the soaked plank(s) dry and place the marinated salmon on top. Place the plank(s) on the grill grate, close the cover, and cook for 10 to 12 minutes, until the salmon is done to your liking. Douse or mist the plank(s) with a bit of water if they catch fire.

7. Spoon the bulgur salad onto serving plates, top with the salmon fillets, and serve.

SOURCING SAVVY

English/hothouse cucumbers are long and slender with tender skin and tiny seeds. They're a little pricier than garden-variety cukes, but you can usually find them on sale in packs of three. They do not need to be peeled.

PRO TIP

Most large supermarkets carry cedar planks near the seafood department during grilling season. They can be reused until they become overly charred; I usually get at least two dinners out of each one; simply scrub them clean and allow them to dry until their next use.

Arugula, Crispy Feta & Watermelon Salad

WITH BALSAMIC VINAIGRETTE

When Michael and I were in our early thirties, our favorite restaurant was Levante's, a Mediterranean place just a stone's throw from our apartment in Bethesda, Maryland. We used to eat outside on the sidewalk patio with our babies napping in their strollers and our Labrador retriever, Miles, keeping watch under the table. How we managed all that I have no idea, but I guess we were pretty desperate to eat out—and oh, how I miss those days when the kids were young! My favorite dish from Levante's was the arugula salad topped with crispy feta. It's easy to prepare at home, and the feta makes the salad substantial enough to serve as a very light meal. If you'd like to bulk it up, grilled steak (see page 159), chicken, or shrimp (see page 39) would all work nicely.

Serves 4

FOR THE VINAIGRETTE

1 tablespoon Dijon mustard

1 tablespoon finely minced shallot (from 1 small shallot)

1 very small garlic clove, finely minced

⅛ teaspoon salt

¼ teaspoon freshly ground black pepper

1½ teaspoons sugar

3 tablespoons balsamic vinegar

½ cup (120 mL) extra-virgin olive oil

FOR THE SALAD

1 (8-ounce/227 g) block feta cheese

¼ cup (33 g) all-purpose flour

1 large egg

⅔ cup (36 g) panko bread crumbs

Vegetable oil, for frying

6 ounces (170 g) baby arugula

2 cups (300 g) medium diced watermelon

1 English/hothouse cucumber, halved, seeded, and cut into ½-inch/13 mm dice

⅓ cup (13 g) roughly chopped fresh mint

MAKE-AHEAD INSTRUCTIONS

The vinaigrette can be made 2 days ahead and refrigerated.

SOURCING SAVVY

I like President-brand chunk feta cheese for this recipe; be sure you don't accidentally pick up the fat-free one, as they are usually sold side by side.

1. Make the vinaigrette: Combine the mustard, shallot, garlic, salt, pepper, sugar, vinegar, and oil in a medium jar with a tight-fitting lid; screw on the lid and shake vigorously to emulsify. (Alternatively, whisk the ingredients together in a bowl.)

2. Make the salad: Carefully slice the feta block in half horizontally so that you have two ½-inch-thick (13 mm) blocks. Cut each block in half diagonally so that you have four ½-inch-thick (13 mm) triangles of feta.

-RECIPE CONTINUES-

3. Set up your breading station. Place the flour on a small plate; beat the egg in a wide, shallow bowl; and place the panko in a separate wide, shallow bowl. Using your hands, coat the feta pieces first in the flour, then dip them in the egg, then coat them with the panko (use one hand for the flour and panko and the other hand for the eggs so it won't be as messy). Place the breaded feta on a paper towel–lined plate.

4. Pour the oil into a small nonstick skillet until it's about ⅛ inch (3 mm) deep. Heat the pan over medium heat until the oil is hot and shimmering. Carefully add the breaded feta to the hot oil (do not crowd the pan; you may need to do this in batches), and fry for 60 to 90 seconds per side, or until golden brown on both sides. Reduce the heat if the feta is browning too quickly. Place the fried feta on a clean paper towel–lined plate to drain any excess oil. Let cool while you assemble the salad.

5. Divide the arugula evenly among 4 serving plates. Top with the watermelon, cucumber, and mint. Drizzle each salad with about 2 tablespoons of the vinaigrette and top with a wedge of crispy feta. Pass the remaining vinaigrette at the table.

Summer Garden Salad

WITH GRILLED SHRIMP & FRESH HERB VINAIGRETTE

I came up with this salad as a way to use up all the herbs and vegetables that grow like wildfire in my garden, but even if you buy all the ingredients at the supermarket, it still tastes amazingly garden fresh. The bright green vinaigrette, packed with fragrant fresh mint and parsley, is the star and brings all the other elements—like plump grilled shrimp, fresh vegetables, tangy feta cheese, and briny Greek olives—together. One of my recipe testers, who owns a winery on the Sonoma Coast in California, described the salad as "a glorious dinner for a summer evening, especially paired with a very crisp, chilled Chardonnay." To warm the pita/flatbread, brush it lightly with olive oil and place it on the grill for a minute while grilling the shrimp.

Serves 4

FOR THE VINAIGRETTE

1 cup (16 g) loosely packed Italian parsley leaves

1 cup (16 g) loosely packed mint leaves

½ teaspoon dried oregano

2 garlic cloves, roughly chopped

⅓ cup (72 mL) white wine vinegar

¾ cup (180 mL) extra-virgin olive oil

Scant 1 teaspoon salt

½ teaspoon freshly ground black pepper

2 teaspoons honey

FOR THE SALAD

8 cups (280 g) chopped romaine lettuce (from 2 hearts)

1 English/hothouse cucumber, seeded and thinly sliced

2 medium carrots, shaved into ribbons (see Pro Tip)

1½ cups (142 g) grape tomatoes, halved (from 1 pint)

½ cup (80 g) pitted Greek olives

¾ cup (90 g) crumbled feta cheese

Warm pita or other flatbread, for serving

FOR THE SHRIMP

2 pounds (907 g) jumbo (16/20) shrimp, peeled and deveined

2 tablespoons extra-virgin olive oil

¼ teaspoon salt

¼ teaspoon freshly ground black pepper

MAKE-AHEAD INSTRUCTIONS

The vinaigrette can be made a day ahead and refrigerated.

SOURCING SAVVY

Ever wondered what those mysterious numbers are when you are purchasing shrimp? They represent the range in the number of shrimp of that size that make up a pound. For example, a package of large shrimp labeled "31/35" indicates that a pound contains anywhere between 31 and 35 shrimp.

PRO TIPS

Always be sure salad greens are dry before dressing them; any moisture will water down the vinaigrette.

—

To shave the carrots into wide ribbons, use a vegetable peeler. Run the peeler away from you, down the length of the carrots, shaving off long ribbons and rotating a few times as you go.

1. Preheat the grill to medium-high heat.

2. Make the vinaigrette: Combine all the vinaigrette ingredients in a food processor and process until smooth and bright green. Set aside.

3. Make the salad: Place the lettuce, cucumber, carrots, tomatoes, and olives in a large bowl. Refrigerate until ready to serve.

-RECIPE CONTINUES-

4. Grill the shrimp: Toss the shrimp with the oil, salt, and pepper. Thread onto skewers, if desired. (I usually don't bother, unless the shrimp are on the smaller side, in which case they might slip through the grill grates.)

5. Using tongs, dip a wad of paper towels in vegetable oil and carefully wipe the grill grate several times until glossy and coated to prevent sticking. Place the shrimp on the grill and cook until plump and slightly charred, 1 to 2 minutes per side. Transfer the cooked shrimp to a bowl and toss with 2 tablespoons of the vinaigrette.

6. Finish the salad: Pull the salad out of the refrigerator. Add about three-quarters of the vinaigrette to the salad and toss well. Add more vinaigrette, little by little, until the salad is dressed to your liking. Toss in the feta cheese, then taste and adjust seasoning if necessary. Transfer the salad to a serving platter or onto plates. Top with the grilled shrimp and serve with warm pita bread, if desired.

Classic Cobb

WITH DIJON VINAIGRETTE

I love salads that have a lot of "stuff" in them, and this classic cobb fits the bill. But what makes it really special is that, instead of using plain poached or grilled chicken, which can be a bit boring, the chicken is cooked in the rendered fat from the bacon—a technique I borrowed from a *New York Times* recipe by Alison Roman. Not only does it add a surprising amount of flavor to the salad, but it also makes full use of all the ingredients. Go ahead and cook some extra bacon; it's impossible to resist the temptation to sneak a few bites while you put the rest of the salad together.

Serves 4 to 6

FOR THE VINAIGRETTE

2 tablespoons finely chopped shallot (from 1 medium shallot)

¼ cup (60 mL) red wine vinegar

½ cup (120 mL) vegetable oil

1 tablespoon Dijon mustard

¾ teaspoon salt

½ teaspoon freshly ground black pepper

¾ teaspoon sugar

FOR THE SALAD

6 slices thick-cut bacon, cut into ½-inch (13 mm) pieces

1 pound (454 g) chicken tenders, cut into ¾-inch (19 mm) pieces

½ teaspoon salt

3 romaine hearts (from one 22-ounce/624 g bag), roughly chopped

1 pint (283 g) grape tomatoes, halved if desired

4 hard-boiled eggs, diced

2 avocados, pitted and diced

½ cup (60 g) crumbled blue cheese (optional)

MAKE-AHEAD INSTRUCTIONS

The vinaigrette can be made 2 days ahead and refrigerated.

SOURCING SAVVY

You can save yourself a step by purchasing packaged hard-boiled eggs at the grocery store (usually found near the fresh eggs).

1. Make the vinaigrette: Combine the shallot, vinegar, oil, mustard, salt, pepper, and sugar in a medium jar with a tight-fitting lid; screw on the lid and shake vigorously to emulsify. (Alternatively, whisk the ingredients together in a bowl.)

2. Make the salad: In a medium nonstick skillet over medium heat, cook the bacon, stirring occasionally, until crisp, 6 to 8 minutes. Use a slotted spoon to transfer the bacon to a paper towel–lined plate to drain, leaving the fat in the pan. Season the chicken with the salt and add to the bacon fat in a single layer; cook the chicken over medium heat, stirring frequently, until cooked through, 3 to 5 minutes. Using the slotted spoon, remove the chicken to a plate and set aside to cool.

-RECIPE CONTINUES-

3. Put the romaine, chicken, and the tomatoes in a large mixing bowl. Give the dressing a shake to re-emulsify, then add three-quarters of it to the bowl; toss gently to combine. Add more dressing, little by little, until the greens are dressed to your liking. Taste and adjust the seasoning if necessary. Arrange the salad on a serving platter or plates.

4. Sprinkle the salad with the hard-boiled eggs, avocados, blue cheese (if using), and reserved bacon. Pass the pepper mill at the table.

HOW TO HARD-BOIL EGGS

Place the eggs in a medium saucepan and fill the pan with enough water so that it is about an inch higher than the eggs. Bring to a boil over high heat, then remove the pan from the heat, cover, and let stand for 12 minutes. Pour the hot water out of the pan and fill it with cold water; let the eggs cool. Tap each egg on the counter to crack the shell, then peel under cold running water.

Pan-Seared Steak, Baby Greens & Roasted Beet Salad

WITH HONEY-DIJON VINAIGRETTE

The base of this salad (the salad *without* the steak) is my go-to dinner party salad. I don't think I've ever served it without sending a few people home with the recipe. It's a bit of a to-do for a weeknight starter, but if you top it with a crusty pan-seared steak, it makes a doable and chic weeknight supper.

Serves 4

FOR THE VINAIGRETTE

2 tablespoons honey

1½ tablespoons Dijon mustard

3 tablespoons red wine vinegar

1½ tablespoons minced shallot (from 1 small shallot)

½ teaspoon salt

¼ teaspoon freshly ground black pepper

6 tablespoons (90 mL) vegetable oil

FOR THE SALAD

2 (12-ounce/340 g) New York strip or rib-eye steaks or 4 (6-ounce/ 170 g) filets mignons

1 teaspoon kosher salt

½ teaspoon freshly ground black pepper

1 tablespoon vegetable oil

10 ounces (284 g) baby greens

8 ounces (227 g) store-bought roasted beets, cut into wedges

¾ cup (105 g) crumbled goat cheese

⅔ cup (80 g) walnuts, toasted (if desired) and coarsely chopped

MAKE-AHEAD INSTRUCTIONS

The vinaigrette can be made 2 days ahead and refrigerated.

SOURCING SAVVY

Feel free to roast your own beets (see page 46), but I typically buy vacuum-packed roasted beets, such as Love Beets, which are available in the produce section of most supermarkets. (Be sure to top the salad with the beets, as opposed to tossing them in; tossing the beets into the salad will turn everything pink.)

1. Make the vinaigrette: Add the honey, mustard, vinegar, shallot, salt, pepper, and oil to a medium jar with a tight-fitting lid; screw on the lid and shake vigorously to emulsify. (Alternatively, whisk the ingredients together in a medium bowl.) Taste and adjust seasoning if necessary.

2. Make the salad: Pat the steaks dry and, if they are thick, gently press them down with the palm of your hand so that they are 1½ inches (4 cm) thick. Season the steaks all over with the kosher salt and pepper.

3. In a medium skillet, heat the oil over medium-high heat. When the oil is hot and shimmering, add the steaks and cook for about 4 minutes on each side, turning only once, for medium-rare (or 5 minutes per side for medium). Transfer the steaks to a cutting board, tent with foil, and let rest for about 5 minutes.

-RECIPE CONTINUES-

4. Place the greens in a large bowl. Drizzle with about half the vinaigrette and toss to coat. Add the remaining vinaigrette, little by little, until the salad is nicely dressed (you may have some vinaigrette left over). Divide the greens evenly among plates, then top with the beets, goat cheese, and walnuts.

5. Slice the steaks crosswise about ¼ inch (6 mm) thick and arrange over or beside the salads.

HOW TO ROAST BEETS

Preheat the oven to 425°F (220°C) and set an oven rack in the middle position. Wipe or scrub the beets clean, then trim the stems down to 1 inch, leaving the "tails" (roots) on. Place the beets on a large piece of heavy-duty aluminum foil, drizzle lightly with olive oil, then wrap the foil around the beets to form a neat packet. Roast directly on the rack until tender, about 1 hour. Test for doneness by piercing the largest beet with the tip of a knife; if the knife enters easily, it's done. Unwrap the beets and let sit until cool enough to handle. Using your hands or a paring knife, peel the skin directly on the foil or a stain-proof cutting board or plate.

Muffuletta Salad
WITH OLIVE VINAIGRETTE

This salad was inspired by *Flavors of the Southern Coast: Cooking with Tommy Bahama*, a gorgeous coffee-table cookbook I picked up in Longboat Key, Florida, where my parents spend the winter. Based on the famous muffuletta sandwiches sold at Central Market in New Orleans, the salad is a bowlful of exciting flavors and textures. There are fresh vegetables—juicy tomatoes, crisp celery, and peppery arugula—along with briny olives, deli meats, cheese, and homemade croutons. It's a fun salad filled with classic New Orleans flavor. Try it!

MAKE-AHEAD
INSTRUCTIONS
The vinaigrette can be made 2 days ahead and refrigerated.

Serves 4

FOR THE OLIVE VINAIGRETTE

3 tablespoons red wine vinegar

½ cup (120 mL) extra-virgin olive oil

½ cup (70 g) good-quality green olives, coarsely chopped

1 small garlic clove, minced

¼ teaspoon salt

¼ teaspoon sugar

¼ teaspoon freshly ground black pepper

FOR THE SALAD

3 tablespoons extra-virgin olive oil

4 cups (227 g) 1-inch (2.5 cm) cubed good-quality Italian bread (from 1 loaf)

1½ cups (210 g) grape tomatoes, halved (from 1 pint)

4 celery stalks, thinly sliced

4 ounces (113 g) sliced Genoa salami or capicola, thinly sliced into bite-sized strips

6 ounces (170 g) sliced ham or mortadella, thinly sliced into bite-sized strips

8 ounces (227 g) sharp Provolone, diced

5 ounces (142 g) baby arugula

1 tablespoon sesame seeds

1. Make the olive vinaigrette: In a large salad bowl, whisk together the vinegar, oil, olives, garlic, salt, sugar, and pepper.

2. Make the salad: Heat the oil over medium-high heat in a large nonstick pan. Add the bread cubes and cook, stirring frequently, until golden outside but still somewhat soft inside, 5 to 6 minutes.

3. To the vinaigrette, add the tomatoes, celery, salami, ham, Provolone, arugula, sesame seeds, and toasted bread. Toss until evenly coated, then taste and adjust the seasoning if necessary. Let the salad stand for about 5 minutes to allow the bread to absorb some of the dressing, then serve.

Soba Chicken Noodle Salad
WITH GINGER PEANUT DRESSING

I used to write a salad column for the popular food website *Serious Eats*. This Asian-inspired noodle salad with chicken, vegetables, and a punchy dressing seasoned with soy sauce, ginger, garlic, and peanut butter was the first recipe I contributed and also the most popular. It is everything you want a summertime meal to be: flavorful, light, and totally satisfying. Note that the dressing will taste acidic and salty before you toss it with the noodles—because the noodles will soak up the flavor quickly, you have to over-season the dressing slightly. Feel free to make the dressing ahead of time, but cook and dress the noodles at the last minute so they don't get soggy.

Serves 4

FOR THE SALAD

10 ounces (285 g) soba noodles

2 cups (260 g) shredded cooked chicken

1 red bell pepper, cut into bite-sized pieces

4 scallions (light and green parts), thinly sliced

½ cup (70 g) chopped salted peanuts

¼ cup (10 g) chopped fresh cilantro

1 tablespoon sesame seeds

FOR THE DRESSING

6 tablespoons (90 mL) soy sauce

3 tablespoons seasoned rice wine vinegar

2 tablespoons peanut oil

1 tablespoon toasted sesame oil

1½ tablespoons creamy peanut butter

2 small garlic cloves, roughly chopped

1 tablespoon minced fresh ginger (from a 1-inch/2.5 cm knob)

1 tablespoon sugar

1. Begin the salad: Bring a large pot of salted water to a boil. Cook the noodles according to the package instructions, stirring occasionally so they don't stick. Drain and rinse well under cold water.

2. Make the dressing: Meanwhile, in a small food processor or blender, combine the soy sauce, vinegar, peanut oil, sesame oil, peanut butter, garlic, ginger, and sugar; blend until smooth.

3. Finish the salad: In a large bowl, toss the noodles with the shredded chicken, bell pepper, scallions, peanuts, cilantro, sesame seeds, and the dressing. Taste and adjust the seasoning if necessary. Serve immediately.

Breakfast for Dinner

Mushroom Gruyère Quiche

Love 'em or hate 'em, people tend to have strong feelings about mushrooms. I am firmly in the love 'em camp, especially when it comes to gourmet mushrooms, like shiitakes, oysters, and porcini. They have an earthy, umami flavor and a meaty texture, and they're a great way to add bulk to vegetarian dishes, like a quiche. For this recipe, it's nice to use a variety of mushrooms; you can usually find a packaged "gourmet" or "chef's sampler" blend in the produce department at the supermarket.

Don't feel guilty about using a store-bought pie crust. A homemade crust is time-consuming to make, and to me, the best part of a quiche is the filling. With a good-quality frozen crust, you can whip up a delicious quiche with very little effort—perfect for a filling yet light-ish weeknight meal. Just be sure to buy a deep-dish crust; a regular pie shell is not deep enough to hold all the filling.

Serves 4 to 6

1 (9-inch/23 cm) deep-dish frozen pie crust (shell)

3 tablespoons unsalted butter

⅔ pound (300 g) mushrooms, stemmed and diced (preferably an assortment of shiitake, oyster, and porcini; see Sourcing Savvy)

⅓ cup (40 g) finely chopped shallot (from 1 medium shallot)

¾ teaspoon salt

2 garlic cloves, minced

2 teaspoons finely chopped fresh thyme, or ½ teaspoon dried

4 large eggs

1¼ cups (300 mL) heavy cream

⅛ teaspoon cayenne pepper

Pinch of ground nutmeg

1¼ cups (5 ounces/150 g) finely shredded Gruyère cheese

HEADS UP

Make sure you use the small holes on your grater to finely grate the Gruyère. If it's not finely grated enough, it won't fully melt.

MAKE-AHEAD/FREEZER-FRIENDLY INSTRUCTIONS

The quiche can be fully prepared up to 1 day ahead and refrigerated, or frozen for up to 3 months. To freeze, after the quiche has cooled to room temperature, wrap it securely with a layer of plastic wrap and then a layer of aluminum foil, making sure to fully seal all the edges. Thaw the frozen quiche in the refrigerator overnight. Reheat, covered with foil, in a 300°F (150°C) oven for 35 to 45 minutes, or until hot in the center.

SOURCING SAVVY

If you purchase your mushrooms already stemmed and sliced, you'll need about ½ pound (227 g) or 3 cups.

1. Preheat the oven to 400°F (205°C) and set an oven rack in the middle position. Remove the pie crust from the freezer and let thaw until just soft enough to easily prick with a fork, about 10 minutes.

2. Prick the bottom and sides of the crust all over with a fork. Place the crust on a baking sheet (this makes it easy to move in and out of the oven) and bake until lightly golden, about 10 minutes. (Keep an eye on it; if it puffs up while cooking, gently prick it with a fork so it deflates.) See Pro Tip if your crust cracks while baking. Set the crust aside and reduce the oven temperature to 325°F (165°C).

3. In a medium nonstick skillet over medium-high heat, melt 2 tablespoons of the butter. Add the mushrooms and cook, stirring frequently, until starting to brown, 4 to 5 minutes. Add the remaining tablespoon butter, the shallots, and ¼ teaspoon of the salt and cook for 2 minutes more. Add the garlic and cook for 1 minute more. Stir in the thyme. Remove the pan from the heat and set aside.

-RECIPE CONTINUES-

4. In a medium bowl, whisk the eggs. Add the cream, cayenne, nutmeg, and the remaining ½ teaspoon salt; whisk until evenly combined.

5. Spread half the mushroom mixture over the bottom of the cooked crust. Top with all the Gruyère and then the remaining mushroom mixture. Pour the egg/cream mixture over the top.

6. Slide the quiche (still on the baking sheet) into the oven and bake for 45 to 55 minutes, until the top is lightly golden and the custard is set. Serve hot or warm.

Eggs in Purgatory

WITH GARLIC TOAST

Similar to Middle Eastern shakshuka or Mexican huevos rancheros, the Southern Italian dish known as eggs in purgatory, or uova in purgatorio, consists of eggs gently poached in a fiery tomato sauce. The origin of the name is a bit of a mystery, but by most accounts, the eggs represent souls suspended in the fiery pits of . . . you know. Fittingly, the dish is considered a soothing morning-after hangover cure. To quote one of my favorite food writers, Nigella Lawson, "Eggs in purgatory is absolute heaven when you're feeling like hell." The dish also works well for dinner, especially paired with garlic toast and a salad or roasted vegetables. What's more, it's an affordable one-skillet meal that you can whip up in a flash from pantry staples.

Serves 3 to 4

3 tablespoons extra-virgin olive oil

3 tablespoons unsalted butter

2 garlic cloves, chopped

¼ teaspoon red pepper flakes, plus more for serving

1 (28-ounce/794 g) can whole peeled plum tomatoes, chopped, with their juices (see Pro Tip)

1 teaspoon salt, plus more for the eggs

1 teaspoon sugar

¼ cup (25 g) finely grated Parmigiano-Reggiano cheese, plus more for serving

6 large eggs

2 tablespoons chopped fresh basil

Garlic toast, for serving (recipe follows)

1. In a large broiler-proof skillet with a lid, heat the oil and butter over medium heat until the butter is melted. Add the garlic and red pepper flakes and cook, stirring constantly, until fragrant, about 1 minute. Do not brown. Add the chopped tomatoes and their juices to the skillet and stir in the salt and sugar. Bring to a boil, then reduce the heat to a lively simmer and cook, uncovered, until the tomatoes break down and thicken into a sauce, 20 to 25 minutes.

2. While the sauce simmers, set an oven rack in the top position and preheat the broiler.

3. Add the Parmigiano-Reggiano to the sauce, then taste and adjust the seasoning if necessary. Using the back of a spoon, make 6 wells in the sauce, and then carefully crack an egg into each well. Sprinkle the eggs with a generous pinch of salt. Reduce the heat to low, cover the pan, and cook until

-RECIPE CONTINUES-

MAKE-AHEAD INSTRUCTIONS

The tomato sauce can be made up to 2 days ahead and refrigerated, or frozen for up to 2 months. Reheat the sauce on the stovetop and proceed with the recipe when ready to serve.

PRO TIP

Diced canned tomatoes are treated with a chemical that prevents them from breaking down when cooking, so when I want a smooth tomato sauce, I prefer to use canned whole tomatoes and chop them myself. You can crush them by hand individually as you add them to the pan, but they splatter like crazy, so it's best to either use kitchen shears to cut them directly in the can or pour the entire contents of the can into a resealable freezer bag, press out any excess air, seal tightly, and then squish by hand.

the egg whites are mostly set but still translucent on top, 3 to 4 minutes. Remove the lid, transfer the pan to the oven, and broil until the eggs are cooked to your liking, 30 seconds to 1 minute for runny yolks. Remove the pan from the oven and place an oven mitt or dish towel over the handle to remind yourself that it's hot. Sprinkle the basil over the top. Serve with the garlic toast, passing more Parmigiano-Reggiano and red pepper flakes at the table.

Garlic Toast

1 baguette, sliced ¾ inch (2 cm) thick on the bias

3 tablespoons extra-virgin olive oil

Salt and freshly ground black pepper

1 garlic clove, halved lengthwise

1. Preheat the broiler and set an oven rack about 5 inches (13 cm) beneath the heating element. Line a 13 × 18-inch (33 × 46 cm) baking sheet with heavy-duty aluminum foil.

2. Arrange the baguette slices on the prepared baking sheet. Brush both sides of the bread with the oil and sprinkle with a pinch of salt and a few grinds of pepper. Broil for 1 to 2 minutes, watching carefully so it doesn't burn, until golden brown on top. Remove the pan from the oven and, using tongs, flip the slices over. Place back under the broiler until golden brown on the second side, 1 to 2 minutes more.

3. Rub each slice with the cut side of the garlic, going back and forth once (or twice, if you like your toast extra garlicky). Set aside until ready to serve.

Sausage & Egg Breakfast Burritos WITH AVOCADO-TOMATO SALSA

These burritos are one of my kids' most requested breakfast-for-dinner dishes. The inspiration for the recipe comes from Lake Anne Market, a hidden-gem bodega in my hometown of Reston, Virginia.

Serves 4

FOR THE SALSA

1 large avocado, pitted and diced

½ cup (75 g) diced seeded ripe tomato (from 1 tomato)

2 tablespoons minced shallot (from 1 small shallot)

1 garlic clove, minced

1 medium jalapeño pepper, seeded and minced

1 tablespoon fresh lime juice (from 1 lime)

½ teaspoon salt

¼ teaspoon ground cumin

¼ cup (10 g) chopped fresh cilantro

FOR THE BURRITOS

4 large eggs

¼ teaspoon smoked paprika

¼ teaspoon salt

½ pound (227 g) spicy sausage (such as fresh chorizo, Italian, or other), removed from casings

4 (10-inch/25 cm) burrito-size flour tortillas

1⅓ cups (160 g) shredded Monterey Jack cheese

Vegetable oil

1. Make the salsa: In a medium bowl, mix the avocado, tomato, shallot, garlic, jalapeño, lime juice, salt, cumin, and cilantro. Taste and adjust the seasoning if necessary.

2. Make the burritos: In a medium bowl, whisk the eggs with the smoked paprika and salt.

3. Heat a large nonstick pan over medium-high heat. Add the sausage and cook, stirring and breaking it up, until browned, 4 to 5 minutes. Use a slotted spoon to transfer the sausage to a plate, leaving the drippings in the pan. Reduce the heat to low. Add the eggs and scramble until just cooked through. Transfer the eggs to a plate. Clean the pan; you'll use it again.

4. Spoon about ¼ cup (50 g) of the salsa onto each tortilla (you'll have a little salsa left over; that's for the cook!), followed by one-fourth of the sausage, one-fourth of the eggs, and ⅓ cup (40 g) of the cheese. Fold the sides of the tortilla over the filling and roll into a burrito, tucking in the edges as you go.

5. Lightly coat the pan with oil and set over medium heat. When the pan is hot, add the burritos, seam side down. Cover and cook until golden brown, about 3 minutes. Flip the burritos and continue cooking, covered, until golden, a few minutes more. Serve warm.

HEADS UP

The avocado-tomato salsa is spicy. If you're making these for kids, consider omitting or reducing the jalapeño pepper (my kids actually prefer the burritos with no salsa at all).

MAKE-AHEAD INSTRUCTIONS

The burritos may be assembled a few hours ahead of time, wrapped tightly in plastic wrap, and refrigerated before cooking.

PRO TIP

To remove the casings from the sausage, use kitchen shears or a paring knife to slice open each link lengthwise. The cut should be shallow enough to just pierce the casing—there's no need to cut all the way through the sausage. Gently pull the casing away and discard. Alternatively, you can just squeeze the meat out of the casing.

Parmesan & Cheddar Soufflé

PRO TIP

Folding is a technique used to mix a light and airy ingredient, like beaten egg whites, into a heavier mixture, like a soufflé base, without deflating the lighter mixture. After combining the two mixtures, use a rubber spatula to cut down to the bottom of the bowl. Pull the spatula toward you, scooping up the contents from the bottom of the bowl, and in one sweeping motion, fold the scooped up portion over the top. Turn the bowl a quarter turn and repeat the motions, scraping the sides of the bowl occasionally, until the ingredients are evenly combined.

When I was an apprentice at L'Auberge Chez Francois, a charming French restaurant right outside of Washington, D.C., one of my jobs was prepping the dessert soufflé dishes for the evening service. It was tedious because there were so many of them. Soufflés are always popular menu items because they have a reputation for being temperamental—heaven forbid you peek into the oven or make a loud noise!—and even confident cooks are nervous to make them at home. But the truth is that soufflés are quite easy to make. I think one thing that makes soufflés feel intimidating is the need for a special soufflé dish, but as you can see, you don't need one here; a 2-quart (2 L) glass or straight-sided ceramic baking dish—even a standard 8-inch (20 cm) square Pyrex pan—will work. Pair the soufflé with a salad (see page 45, without the steak) for a light and elegant meal that will wow your family (they don't need to know how easy it is!).

Serves 4

3 tablespoons unsalted butter, plus softened butter for greasing the pan

½ cup (50 g) finely grated Parmigiano-Reggiano cheese

3 tablespoons all-purpose flour

1 cup (240 mL) whole milk, cold

¼ teaspoon salt

¼ teaspoon freshly ground black pepper

Pinch of ground nutmeg

1½ cups (6 ounces/180 g) shredded good-quality sharp Cheddar cheese

4 large egg yolks (save the whites)

2 tablespoons finely chopped chives

5 large egg whites

¼ teaspoon cream of tartar

1. Preheat the oven to 350°F (175°C) and set an oven rack in the middle position.

2. Use softened butter to grease a 2-quart/2 L (8-inch/20 cm) soufflé or ceramic casserole dish. Add ¼ cup (25 g) of the Parmigiano-Reggiano and roll it around the dish to coat the bottom and sides.

3. In a small saucepan over medium heat, melt the 3 tablespoons butter. Add the flour and cook, whisking constantly, for about 1 minute. Add the milk and whisk the mixture until smooth. Continue cooking, whisking constantly, until the mixture thickens and comes to a boil, a few minutes (be sure to scrape the edges of the pan with your whisk, where the mixture thickens first). Remove the pan from the heat and stir in the salt, pepper, and nutmeg. Add the Cheddar and the remaining ¼ cup (25 g) Parmigiano-Reggiano; stir until the cheeses are melted and the mixture is thick and smooth. Let cool for 10 minutes, then whisk in the egg yolks and chives.

4. In the bowl of an electric mixer fitted with the whisk or beaters, whip the egg whites and cream of tartar on medium-low speed until foamy, about 1 minute. Increase the speed to medium high and whip until stiff peaks form, about 3 minutes. Add one-third of the cooled milk/cheese mixture to the whites and beat on medium speed until smooth. Add the remaining milk mixture to the whites and, using a rubber spatula, fold until uniform (see Pro Tip).

5. Pour the batter into the prepared soufflé or casserole dish (it should come about 1 inch/2.5 cm from the top; if you have extra batter, discard it or bake it in a separate dish). Place the dish on a baking sheet and slide it into the oven. (The baking sheet just makes it easier to move in and out of the oven.) Bake for about 35 minutes, or until puffed and golden brown on top. The soufflé will stay inflated for a while, but it is best to serve it immediately.

Croque Monsieur

Made from simple ingredients commonly found in any French home, a croque monsieur is a Frenchified grilled ham-and-cheese sandwich. The name is based on the verb croquer ("to crunch") and the word monsieur ("mister"), but according to my French brother-in-law, Guillaume, it just means "the best grilled cheese ever." The sandwich is filled and topped with a mustard-flavored béchamel sauce, which makes it tangy, rich, and deliciously salty. Pair it with an ice-cold beer or a crisp white wine. A green salad goes nicely, too. And if you add a fried egg on top, it becomes a croque madame!

PRO TIP

If you have one, a flat whisk is ideal for whisking the ingredients for the cheese sauce. Its semi-flat shape makes it easier to get into the corners of the saucepan.

Serves 6

2 tablespoons unsalted butter

2 tablespoons all-purpose flour

1½ cups (360 mL) whole milk

2 cups (8 ounces/240 g) shredded Gruyère cheese

1½ tablespoons Dijon mustard

Scant ½ teaspoon salt

¼ teaspoon freshly ground black pepper

Pinch of ground nutmeg

12 (½ inch/13 mm thick) slices crusty Italian or French sandwich bread

10 ounces (300 g) thinly sliced Black Forest ham

1. Preheat the oven to 425°F (220°C) and set 2 oven racks in the centermost positions.

2. In a small saucepan over medium heat, melt the butter. Add the flour and cook, whisking constantly, until the mixture foams and subsides, about 1 minute. Add the milk and whisk until smooth. Continue cooking, whisking constantly, until the mixture thickens and comes to a boil, a few minutes. Lower the heat to medium low and cook, stirring frequently, until the mixture is thick enough to coat the back of a spoon, about 3 minutes. Off the heat, add ½ cup (60 g) of the Gruyère and stir until melted. Add the mustard, salt, pepper, and nutmeg and whisk to combine. Set aside. The sauce will thicken as it cools.

3. Meanwhile, toast the bread. Place the bread slices on two 13 × 18-inch (33 × 46 cm) baking sheets and bake for 6 to 8 minutes, flipping once, until lightly golden.

4. Move an oven rack to the middle position. Line a 13 × 18-inch (33 × 46 cm) baking sheet with parchment paper for easy cleanup.

5. Arrange half of the toasted bread on the baking sheet. Spoon half the cheese sauce over the bread. Arrange the ham slices over the sauce and sprinkle with half the remaining Gruyère. Top with the remaining bread. Spoon the remaining sauce over the bread, letting it drip down the sides of each sandwich, and sprinkle the remaining Gruyère over the top. Bake until bubbling and golden, 15 to 20 minutes. Use a spatula to transfer the sandwiches to plates; serve with forks and knives.

Spinach Frittata

**FREEZER-FRIENDLY
INSTRUCTIONS**

The frittata can be made 2
days ahead and refrigerated,
or frozen for up to 3 months.
If frozen, thaw in the
refrigerator overnight.
Reheat it in the microwave
or, covered with foil, in a
300°F (150°C) oven until
hot in the center.

Filled with heaps of baby spinach and two kinds of cheese, Cheddar and
Parmigiano-Reggiano, this frittata tastes nutritious and rich at the same
time. It's silkier and more quiche-like than most frittatas, which are usually
just glorified omelets with the fillings mixed in rather than stuffed inside.
The key to the delicate texture is adding heavy cream and lots of cheese to
the egg mixture. It's also important to bake the frittata in a low-temperature
oven, as opposed to the traditional stovetop-to-broiler method, so the eggs
cook gently into a custard without scrambling. The frittata can be served
for brunch, lunch, or a light dinner. And since it's good warm or at room
temperature, leftovers can be packed for lunch or taken on a picnic.

Serves 4

2 tablespoons extra-virgin olive oil

¾ cup (90 g) thinly sliced shallot
(from 2 large shallots)

5 ounces (142 g) baby spinach
(5 packed cups)

½ teaspoon salt

8 large eggs

⅓ cup (80 mL) heavy cream

¼ teaspoon freshly ground
black pepper

¾ cup (3 ounces/90 g) shredded
Cheddar cheese

½ cup (50 g) finely grated
Parmigiano-Reggiano cheese

¼ cup (10 g) chopped fresh basil

1. Preheat the oven to 325°F (165°C) and set an oven rack in the middle
position.

2. Heat the oil in a 10-inch (25 cm) ovenproof nonstick skillet over medium
heat. Add the shallots and cook, stirring frequently, until softened, 3 to
4 minutes. Do not brown. Add half the spinach and cook until wilted, about
1 minute. Add the remaining spinach and ¼ teaspoon of the salt and continue
cooking until all the spinach is wilted, 1 to 2 minutes more.

3. In a large bowl, whisk together the eggs, cream, pepper, and the remaining
¼ teaspoon salt.

4. Add the cooked spinach and the Cheddar, Parmigiano-Reggiano, and basil
to the egg mixture and stir to combine. Pour the mixture back into the skillet
(no need to wash it), transfer to the oven, and bake until set, 20 to 23 minutes.
Immediately place an oven mitt over the pan handle to remind yourself that
it is hot (it's easy to forget and burn your hand, and the handle stays hot for a
long time).

5. Serve the frittata directly from the pan, or use a rubber spatula to loosen
the edges and slide the frittata onto a serving platter.

No Fork Needed

Oven-Roasted Chicken Shawarma

MAKE-AHEAD
INSTRUCTIONS

The sauce can be
made 2 days ahead and
refrigerated.

PRO TIP

Chicken thighs need to be
trimmed before you cook
them. Using scissors, simply
cut off any gristle, large
chunks of fat (small bits
will mostly melt away in the
oven), and excess skin. For
those who don't like dark
meat, chicken tenders can be
used, although they won't be
quite as rich and juicy. Note
that tenders will cook about
10 minutes faster than thighs,
so remove them from the
oven after about 25 minutes
while the onion finishes
cooking.

I fell in love with shawarma when I was a student living on a shoestring budget and traveling around Israel in the nineties. A popular Middle Eastern street food, shawarma is made from highly seasoned chicken or lamb stacked in a cone shape and roasted on a slowly turning vertical spit (shawarma is Arabic for "turning"). The meat is shaved to order and piled into pillowy flatbread along with lots of fresh toppings. It's a tough dish to replicate at home, but this oven-roasted chicken version, inspired by my friend Chef Sylvia Fountaine, from the beautiful blog *Feasting at Home*, comes pretty darn close. Tossed with roasted onions and drizzled with a garlicky yogurt sauce, the chicken is juicy and packed with flavor.

Instead of making wraps, you can serve the chicken over rice or a salad. Though the ingredient list looks long, this is an easy weeknight dinner, and it's an enthusiastic favorite among my recipe testers and family alike.

• PHOTOGRAPH ON PAGE 68

Serves 4 to 6

FOR THE CHICKEN

5 tablespoons (74 mL) extra-virgin olive oil

1½ teaspoons salt

2 teaspoons ground cumin

2 teaspoons ground coriander

¾ teaspoon ground turmeric

¼ teaspoon cayenne pepper

Scant ⅛ teaspoon ground cinnamon

2 garlic cloves, minced

2¼ pounds (1 kg) boneless, skinless chicken thighs, trimmed of excess fat

1 large yellow onion, sliced ½ inch (13 mm) thick

FOR THE SAUCE

¾ cup (180 g) plain whole-milk Greek yogurt (okay to substitute 2%)

¼ cup (60 g) best-quality mayonnaise, such as Hellmann's or Duke's

1 tablespoon fresh lemon juice (from 1 lemon)

1 small garlic clove, minced

¼ teaspoon salt

FOR SERVING

6 pieces good-quality flatbread, such as naan or pita

1 small English/hothouse cucumber, halved, seeded, and thinly sliced

2 ripe plum tomatoes, thinly sliced

1. Preheat the oven to 425°F (220°C) and set an oven rack in the middle position. Line a baking sheet with heavy-duty aluminum foil.

2. Make the chicken: In a large bowl, whisk together 3 tablespoons of the oil, 1¼ teaspoons of the salt, the cumin, coriander, turmeric, cayenne, cinnamon, and garlic. Add the chicken and toss to coat evenly. Transfer the chicken to the prepared baking sheet.

3. To the same bowl (no need to rinse it out), add the remaining 2 tablespoons oil, the remaining ¼ teaspoon salt, and the onion; toss until the onion is thoroughly coated. Transfer the onion to the prepared baking sheet, arranging it around the chicken in a single layer.

4. Roast for about 35 minutes, stirring halfway through, until the chicken is cooked through and the onion is softened and starting to brown.

5. Make the sauce: Meanwhile, in a small bowl, whisk together the yogurt, mayonnaise, lemon juice, garlic, and salt. Taste and adjust the seasoning if necessary.

6. Serve the chicken: When the chicken is done, leave the oven on and place the flatbread directly on the rack to warm for a few minutes.

7. Slice the chicken into 1-inch-thick (2.5 cm) strips and then toss it in the pan with the onion and juices. Transfer the chicken and onion, along with any juices, to a serving platter. Serve with the warm flatbread, the yogurt sauce, and the cucumber and tomatoes, and let everyone assemble individual wraps.

Chipotle Shrimp & Poblano Quesadillas

SOURCING SAVVY

Canned chipotle peppers in adobo sauce are small dried, and smoked ripened jalapeño peppers that are packed in a spicy, smoky tomato sauce. You can find them in most supermarkets. Once you open a can, you can transfer any remaining peppers to a plastic or glass container and store them in the refrigerator for up to a month, or freeze them in a resealable freezer bag for up to 6 months.

PRO TIP

These quesadillas have a nice kick to them. If you'd like to make them milder, cut back on the chipotles in adobo sauce.

The inspiration for this recipe comes from Mexican chef Pati Jinich, who makes a pan-fried taco version of this dish, called Governor Shrimp Tacos, that I love. For me, making individual tacos is a bit labor-intensive for a weeknight dinner, so I tweaked her recipe to make larger quesadillas instead. To save time, go ahead and use pre-shredded cheese from a bag; just be sure it's a quality brand, like Tillamook thick-cut Cheddar. You can fit only one quesadilla in the skillet at a time, so feel free to use two pans if you want to speed up the process.

Serves 4

4 tablespoons (½ stick/2 ounces/ 56 g) unsalted butter

1 medium yellow onion, finely chopped

1 poblano pepper, finely diced

3 garlic cloves, minced

1 large ripe tomato, seeded and diced

2 tablespoons minced canned chipotle peppers in adobo sauce, plus 1 tablespoon of the sauce

1½ teaspoons Worcestershire sauce

¾ teaspoon ground cumin

Scant ½ teaspoon salt

⅔ pound (302 g) large (31/35) shrimp, peeled and deveined, chopped into ½-inch (13 mm) pieces

¼ cup (10 g) chopped fresh cilantro

1 tablespoon fresh lime juice (from 1 lime)

4 (10-inch/25 cm) flour tortillas

3 cups (12 ounces/360 g) shredded mild Cheddar cheese

1. Melt 2 tablespoons of the butter in a large nonstick skillet over medium heat. Add the onion and poblano and cook, stirring occasionally, until softened, 3 to 5 minutes. Add the garlic and cook, stirring constantly, for about 1 minute. Add the tomato, chipotles and adobo sauce, Worcestershire sauce, cumin, and salt. Cook, stirring occasionally, for 2 minutes. Add the shrimp and cook, stirring frequently, until they are opaque, 2 to 3 minutes. Stir in the cilantro and lime juice, then taste and adjust the seasoning if necessary. Transfer the mixture to a large bowl. Clean the skillet and return it to the stove.

2. Melt ½ tablespoon of the butter in the skillet over medium heat. Place 1 tortilla in the skillet and toast until slightly puffed in spots, 30 to 60 seconds. Flip the tortilla over and sprinkle evenly with ¾ cup (90 g) of the cheese, leaving a ½-inch (13 mm) border. Spread one-fourth of the shrimp and vegetable mixture over half the tortilla. When the cheese is mostly melted, fold the tortilla over to cover the filling and form a half-moon shape. Cook until the tortilla is crisp and golden and the cheese is fully melted, adjusting the heat as necessary, 1 to 2 minutes per side. Repeat with the remaining ingredients, adjusting the heat as necessary. (Loosely cover the cooked quesadillas with foil to keep them warm.) Let the quesadillas rest a few minutes to allow the filling to set, then cut them into wedges.

Crispy Fried Chicken Sandwiches

While I was writing this book, my daughter, who occasionally grows weary of being my guinea pig taste tester, challenged me to come up with a mash-up version of her favorite fast-food crispy chicken sandwiches (yes, I'm talking about Chick-fil-A and Popeyes). This mission involved several trips to the drive-through, four quarts of oil, a mountain of fried chicken sandwiches, and exhaustive critiques from my kids and their friends (aka the experts). It took me a while, but I finally cracked the code. All I can say is, get ready to be showered with praise—your family will be talking about these for days.

Makes 6 sandwiches

FOR THE CHICKEN

3 boneless, skinless chicken breasts (about 1⅓ pounds/605 g)

2 cups (480 mL) cold water

2 tablespoons plus ¾ teaspoon salt

2 teaspoons sugar

4 to 6 cups (1 to 1.4 L) vegetable or peanut oil, for frying

1 large egg

½ cup (120 mL) milk

1½ cups (195 g) all-purpose flour

3 tablespoons cornstarch

1½ teaspoons baking powder

¾ teaspoon garlic powder

1 tablespoon freshly ground black pepper

1 teaspoon Accent flavor enhancer (also known as MSG)

1 teaspoon paprika

FOR THE SAUCE

½ cup (120 g) best-quality mayonnaise, such as Hellmann's or Duke's

3 tablespoons store-bought barbecue sauce

2 teaspoons Dijon mustard

FOR THE SANDWICHES

6 hamburger buns

Bread-and-butter pickles

HEADS UP

Allow at least 4 hours to brine the chicken.

MAKE-AHEAD INSTRUCTIONS

The sauce can be made 3 days ahead and refrigerated.

SOURCING SAVVY

Accent is an MSG flavor enhancer that brings out the savory, umami flavors of foods. I love the flavor it adds, but if you prefer, you can omit it and increase the salt in the breading to 1 heaping teaspoon.

PRO TIPS

Leftover chicken can be reheated on a foil-lined baking sheet in a 350°F (175°C) oven until hot and crispy, 10 to 15 minutes.

—

A deep-frying thermometer isn't a must, but it really does help maintain the proper temperature for frying, which ensures that the breading is crispy and sticks to the chicken.

1. Make the chicken: One at a time, place the chicken breasts in a resealable freezer bag; using a meat mallet or rolling pin, pound them to an even ¼-inch (6 mm) thickness. Cut each pounded breast in half. (If the pieces seem too large to fit in a bun, trim off the pointy ends; you can cook those as chicken nuggets at the same time you're cooking the breasts.)

2. Pour the cold water into a medium bowl; add the 2 tablespoons of salt and the sugar and whisk until dissolved. Place the chicken breasts in the brine, cover the bowl, and refrigerate for at least 4 hours or overnight (the longer you brine, the saltier the chicken will be).

-RECIPE CONTINUES-

3. Line a plate with a few layers of paper towels and set it next to the stove. Pour the oil into a large, high-sided pot or Dutch oven until it reaches a depth of about 1 inch (2.5 cm). Heat the oil over medium-high heat until shimmering (about 350°F/175°C). (If the end of a wooden spoon or a cube of bread sizzles vigorously when you dip it in, the oil is hot enough.)

4. In a medium bowl, whisk the egg and milk until evenly combined.

5. In another medium bowl, whisk the flour, cornstarch, baking powder, garlic powder, pepper, Accent, paprika, and the remaining ¾ teaspoon salt. Drizzle 4 tablespoons of the egg mixture into the flour mixture and mix with a fork until the flour mixture is evenly clumpy.

6. Line a baking sheet with aluminum foil for easy cleanup. Remove the chicken from the brine and pat dry with paper towels. One at a time, dip each piece into the egg mixture, letting any excess drip off, and then into the flour mixture, turning a few times and pressing firmly so that the clumps adhere. Set the breaded chicken on the lined baking sheet and repeat with the remaining pieces.

7. Carefully place a few pieces of breaded chicken into the hot oil without crowding the pot. Cook, turning a few times, until golden brown and crispy on both sides, 4 to 5 minutes total. Place the cooked chicken on the paper towel–lined plate to drain. Fry the remaining breasts in the same manner, adjusting the heat as necessary to maintain the temperature of the oil.

8. Make the sauce: In a small bowl, whisk together the mayonnaise, barbecue sauce, and mustard.

9. Assemble the sandwiches: Spread some of the sauce on each top and bottom bun. Top each bottom bun with a piece of crispy chicken and a few pickles. Close the sandwiches and serve immediately.

Blackened Fish Tacos

WITH PICKLED ONIONS & LIME CREMA

To me, fish tacos are the ultimate good-mood food. I mean, is there anything like warm corn tortillas overflowing with pan-seared fresh fish—boldly seasoned with chile powder, herbs, and other spices—creamy avocado, crunchy cabbage, and tangy pickled onions to get you in a laid-back, summer state of mind? I use cod here, as it is widely available and affordable, but any flaky white fish will work. Don't be intimidated by the long list of ingredients; this recipe comes together quickly.

Serves 4 (12 tacos)

MAKE-AHEAD INSTRUCTIONS

The pickled onions can be made up to 2 weeks ahead and refrigerated. The crema can be made 2 days ahead and refrigerated.

SOURCING SAVVY

I recommend using Mission brand "super-soft" corn tortillas.

FOR THE PICKLED ONIONS

1 cup (240 mL) cider vinegar

⅓ cup (67 g) sugar

1 teaspoon salt

1 small red onion, sliced ⅛ inch (3 mm) thick

FOR THE FISH

3 tablespoons olive oil

1 teaspoon ancho chile powder

½ teaspoon smoked paprika

¾ teaspoon dried oregano

½ teaspoon ground cumin

⅛ teaspoon cayenne pepper

¾ teaspoon salt

1½ pounds (680 g) cod or similar flaky white fish, cut into 3-inch (8 cm) chunks

FOR THE CREMA

½ cup (120 g) sour cream

½ cup (120 g) best-quality mayonnaise, such as Hellmann's or Duke's

1 small garlic clove, minced

⅛ teaspoon salt

1 to 2 tablespoons fresh lime juice (from 1 lime)

FOR ASSEMBLING

12 (6-inch/15 cm) corn tortillas, warmed according to package instructions

2 cups (120 g) shredded green or red cabbage

1 large avocado, pitted and sliced

Cilantro sprigs (optional)

1. Make the pickled onions: Put the vinegar, sugar, and salt in a medium jar and cover with a lid; shake until the sugar and salt are dissolved. (Alternatively, whisk the mixture in a bowl.) Add the sliced onion, making sure it is mostly submerged (it will relax a bit as it soaks), and set aside for at least 30 minutes or refrigerate for up to 2 weeks. (If using a bowl, cover tightly with plastic wrap.)

2. Marinate the fish: In a medium bowl, whisk together the oil, chile powder, smoked paprika, oregano, cumin, cayenne, and salt. Add the fish and turn to coat evenly. Allow it to marinate while you prepare the rest of the recipe.

-RECIPE CONTINUES-

3. Make the crema: In a small bowl, whisk together the sour cream, mayonnaise, garlic, salt, and 1 tablespoon of the lime juice. Taste and add more lime juice if needed.

4. Cook the fish: Heat a nonstick skillet over medium-high heat. Remove the fish from the marinade and place in the hot pan (there is no need to add oil). Cook the fish undisturbed until nicely blackened on the first side, 3 to 4 minutes. Flip the fish over, reduce the heat to medium, and cook until the fish flakes nicely with a fork, about 2 minutes more. Remove the pan from the heat and flake the fish right in the pan with a fork.

5. Assemble the tacos: Place a generous spoonful of the flaked fish onto the center of a tortilla. Top with pickled onions, crema, the cabbage, avocado, and cilantro sprigs (if using).

Ginger Pork Sliders

WITH TANGY SLAW & SPICY MAYO

These Asian dumpling–inspired sliders are juicy little flavor bombs. They make a fun light dinner and are also a great option for happy hour. If you're not in the mood for sliders, you can shape the meat into 4 or 5 larger burgers—or omit the buns and serve the patties and slaw in lettuce cups or over rice.

Serves 4 to 5

1 (10-ounce/283 g) bag shredded cabbage, preferably red (4 cups)

3 tablespoons rice wine vinegar

1½ tablespoons sugar

3 tablespoons vegetable oil

3 tablespoons soy sauce

2½ teaspoons toasted sesame oil

⅔ cup (32 g) thinly sliced scallions (light and dark green parts; from 1 bunch)

5 tablespoons (13 g) chopped fresh mint

2 tablespoons finely grated ginger (from a 2-inch/5 cm knob)

3 garlic cloves, minced

1½ pounds (680 g) ground pork

⅔ cup (160 g) best-quality mayonnaise, such as Hellmann's or Duke's

2 to 4 tablespoons Asian chili-garlic sauce, to taste

10 slider buns, toasted

HEADS UP

Some of the same ingredients are repeated in the slaw and the sliders, so be sure to read the recipe carefully before getting started.

MAKE-AHEAD/FREEZER-FRIENDLY INSTRUCTIONS

The patties can be formed, covered, and refrigerated up to 1 day ahead of time, or frozen for up to 3 months; if frozen, defrost in the refrigerator overnight.

1. In a large bowl, combine the cabbage, vinegar, sugar, 1 tablespoon of the vegetable oil, 1 tablespoon of the soy sauce, 1 teaspoon of the sesame oil, ¼ cup (13 g) of the scallions, and 2 tablespoons of the mint. Toss well to combine. Let sit on the countertop while you prepare the sliders; the vegetables should soften a bit as they sit.

2. In another large bowl, combine the remaining 2 tablespoons soy sauce, the remaining 1½ teaspoons sesame oil, the remaining scallions, the remaining 3 tablespoons mint, and the ginger, and garlic. Mix to combine. Add the pork and, using your hands, mix until evenly combined. The mixture will be a bit wet; that's okay. Shape the pork mixture into 10 patties slightly wider than the diameter of the slider buns. With your thumb, form a slight depression in the center of each patty to prevent the burgers from puffing up in the pan. Refrigerate until ready to cook.

3. In a small bowl, whisk together the mayonnaise and 2 tablespoons of the chili-garlic sauce. Taste and add more chili sauce to kick up the heat if desired.

4. In a large (12-inch/30 cm) nonstick pan, heat the remaining 2 tablespoons vegetable oil over medium-high heat. Cook the patties, without touching, until golden brown on the first side, about 3 minutes. Flip the patties, reduce the heat to medium, and continue cooking until they are cooked through, 3 to 5 minutes more. Serve the sliders on buns, topped with the slaw and spicy mayo. Pass the remaining slaw on the side.

Chorizo-Style Burgers

WITH SPICED KETCHUP

I can't think of many things that are easier to make than burgers, or many things that my family enjoys more. Popular in Miami and Latin America, chorizo burgers are typically made with a combination of fresh chorizo—a spicy and highly seasoned pork sausage used in Mexican and Spanish cuisine—and ground beef. Fresh chorizo can be hard to find where I live, so I get a similar effect by adding ground pork and spices to my ground beef mixture. With cheese inside and out, these burgers are drip-down-your-chin juicy and packed with flavor. You need to cook the burgers to medium-well because they contain pork; don't worry, though, they will still be tender thanks to the addition of a *panade*, a milk-and-bread paste that helps the meat retain moisture.

Serves 6

FOR THE BURGERS

1 slice white sandwich bread, crust removed, cut into ¼-inch (6 mm) pieces

3 tablespoons milk

1¼ teaspoons salt

1½ teaspoons smoked paprika

1 teaspoon ground cumin

½ teaspoon cayenne pepper

2 teaspoons Worcestershire sauce

2 large garlic cloves, minced

1 pound (454 g) 85% lean ground beef

1 pound (454 g) ground pork

3 scallions (light and dark green parts), very thinly sliced

1 cup (4 ounces/120 g) shredded Monterey Jack cheese or mild Cheddar cheese

6 slices Monterey Jack cheese or mild Cheddar cheese, for topping the burgers

6 hamburger buns, split

Toppings of choice

FOR THE SPICED KETCHUP

1 cup (260 g) ketchup

1 tablespoon cider vinegar

1 teaspoon Worcestershire sauce

1 tablespoon dark or light brown sugar

¼ teaspoon ground cumin

¼ teaspoon smoked paprika

⅛ teaspoon cayenne pepper

1. Preheat the grill to high heat.

2. Make the burgers: In a large bowl, combine the bread, milk, salt, smoked paprika, cumin, cayenne, Worcestershire, and garlic. Using a fork, mash into a smooth paste.

3. Add the beef, pork, scallions, and shredded cheese. Using your hands, mix until evenly combined. The mixture may seem a bit wet; that's normal. Shape the meat mixture into 6 patties about 4 inches (10 cm) in diameter and 1 inch (2.5 cm) thick. Form a slight depression in the center of each patty to prevent the burgers from puffing up on the grill.

4. Make the spiced ketchup: Whisk together the ketchup, vinegar, Worcestershire, sugar, cumin, smoked paprika, and cayenne in a small saucepan over low heat. Simmer, uncovered, for about 5 minutes, or until slightly thickened. Transfer to a small serving bowl.

5. Grill and serve the burgers: Using tongs, dip a wad of paper towels in vegetable oil and carefully wipe the grill grate several times to prevent sticking (since the burgers are on the wet side, it's important to grease the grate well). Grill the burgers, covered, until nicely browned on the first side, 4 to 5 minutes. Flip the burgers and continue cooking for 3 minutes more. Top the burgers with the sliced cheese, close the lid, and cook until the cheese is melted and the burgers are cooked through, about 1 minute more. (These burgers should be cooked to at least medium; they will not dry out. Also, note that they are prone to flare-ups, so keep an eye on them as they cook, and adjust the heat accordingly.) Toast the buns on the cooler side of the grill, if desired. Assemble the burgers and pass the toppings and sauce on the side.

Ciabatta Pesto Pizza

I have tried over and over again to make good pizza using store-bought pizza dough, but I can never get that airy interior and crisp-on-the-bottom crust I want. But you know what does make a fabulous store-bought pizza crust? Ciabatta bread—no rolling pin required! Sliced in half and topped with sauce and cheese, ciabatta bread makes a toasty, pillowy, deep dish–like pizza crust that requires no kneading, proofing, or shaping.

Serves 4

1 (1-pound/454 g) loaf ciabatta bread, sliced in half horizontally

½ cup (120 mL) homemade pesto sauce (recipe follows), plus more for drizzling

8 ounces (227 g) fresh mozzarella cheese, thinly sliced

¼ cup (25 g) finely grated Parmigiano-Reggiano cheese

Handful of basil leaves, torn

Red pepper flakes, for serving (optional)

MAKE-AHEAD/FREEZER FRIENDLY INSTRUCTIONS
If you aren't using the pesto immediately, store in a tightly sealed jar or airtight plastic container, covered with a thin layer of oil (the oil seals out the air and prevents the pesto from oxidizing, which would turn it an unappetizing brown color). The pesto will keep in the refrigerator for about a week, or it can be frozen for up to 3 months.

1. Preheat the oven to 425°F (220°C) and set an oven rack in the middle position. Line a 13 x 18-inch (33 x 46 cm) baking sheet with aluminum foil for easy cleanup.

2. Place the ciabatta halves on the prepared baking sheet, cut side up. Spread the pesto evenly over the bread. Bake the ciabatta halves for 5 minutes.

3. Remove the pan from the oven. Top the bread with the mozzarella and scatter the Parmigiano-Reggiano over the top. Bake for 7 to 9 minutes more, until the cheese is melted and the bread is nicely toasted and crisp on the bottom. Remove from the oven and top with the torn basil and dabs of pesto. Slice and serve with red pepper flakes, if desired.

Pesto Sauce   Makes 1 cup (240 mL)

⅓ cup (40 g) pine nuts or walnuts

2 large garlic cloves, roughly chopped

2 cups (64 g) packed basil leaves

½ teaspoon salt

¼ teaspoon freshly ground black pepper

⅔ cup (160 mL) extra-virgin olive oil, plus more for storing

½ cup (50 g) finely grated Parmigiano-Reggiano cheese

In a food processor, pulse the nuts and garlic until coarsely chopped. Add the basil, salt, and pepper and process until the mixture resembles a paste, about 1 minute. With the processor running, slowly pour the oil through the feed tube and process until the pesto is thoroughly blended. Add the Parmigiano-Reggiano and process 1 minute more.

Ciabatta Pepperoni Pizza

PRO TIP
Cut into small squares, these "pizzas" make fun appetizers for a get-together.

Since my kids prefer more traditional pizza toppings, I usually make them a red sauce and pepperoni version of the Ciabatta pesto pizza on the previous page. If you grew up on Stouffer's French Bread Pizzas as I did, these pepperoni "pizzas" will taste very familiar. I use a good-quality store-bought pizza sauce, such as Rao's, but if you have your own homemade sauce, by all means use it.

Serves 4

1 (1-pound/454 g) loaf ciabatta bread, sliced in half horizontally

¼ cup (60 mL) olive oil

1 large garlic clove, minced

½ cup (120 mL) store-bought or homemade pizza sauce

1 teaspoon dried oregano

8 ounces (227 g) fresh mozzarella, thinly sliced

¼ cup (25 g) finely grated Parmigiano-Reggiano cheese

10 medium slices pepperoni

Salt and freshly ground black pepper

Red pepper flakes (optional)

1. Preheat the oven to 425°F (220°C) and set an oven rack in the middle position. Line a baking sheet with aluminum foil for easy cleanup.

2. Place the ciabatta halves on the prepared baking sheet, cut side up. In a small bowl, mix the oil and garlic, then drizzle evenly over the bread. Spoon the pizza sauce over the top and sprinkle with the oregano. Bake the ciabatta halves for 5 minutes.

3. Remove the pan from the oven. Scatter the mozzarella over the bread and top with the Parmigiano-Reggiano and pepperoni. Bake until the cheese is melted and the bread is nicely toasted and crisp on the bottom, 7 to 9 minutes more. Remove from the oven and sprinkle with a pinch of salt, a few grinds of pepper, and some red pepper flakes, if using.

Pasta, Noodles & Risotto

Summer Pasta Primavera

I realize the title of this dish is a bit of an oxymoron; the word *primavera* means "springtime" in Italian. But, generally, when we think of pasta primavera, we think of pasta with a chorus of vegetables from any season. With roasted tomatoes, corn, and zucchini, this dish is an ode to summer. It's rich in flavor, so I serve it as a main course, but it also makes a fantastic side to grilled Italian sausage. • PHOTOGRAPH ON PAGE 88

Serves 4

2 pints (566 g) cherry or grape tomatoes, halved

4 medium shallots, thinly sliced

5 garlic cloves, smashed

¼ cup (60 mL) extra-virgin olive oil, plus more for serving

2 teaspoons salt

1½ teaspoons sugar

1 medium zucchini, cut into ¼-inch (6 mm) chunks

1½ cups (240 g) fresh corn kernels (from 2 ears)

12 ounces (340 g) fusilli or similar shape pasta

3 tablespoons unsalted butter

1 teaspoon herbes de Provence

⅛ teaspoon red pepper flakes

½ cup (50 g) finely grated pecorino Romano cheese, plus more for serving

½ cup (16 g) tightly packed basil leaves, roughly chopped

⅓ cup (40 g) pine nuts, toasted (see Pro Tip)

1. Preheat the oven to 450°F (235°C). Line a baking sheet with heavy-duty aluminum foil.

2. Combine the tomatoes, shallots, garlic, oil, salt, and sugar on the prepared baking sheet. Toss with your hands or a rubber spatula until the vegetables are evenly coated with oil. Spread the vegetables into a single layer and roast for 15 to 20 minutes, until the tomatoes are just starting to brown. Remove the pan from the oven and add the zucchini and corn. Toss with a rubber spatula (the tomatoes will collapse; that's okay) and spread into an even layer. Roast for 5 minutes more, until the zucchini and corn are crisp-tender.

3. Meanwhile, bring a large pot of salted water to a boil. Cook the pasta until al dente. Drain, then place the pasta back in the pan. Add the roasted vegetables and all their juices to the pan, along with the butter, herbes de Provence, red pepper flakes, pecorino Romano, basil, and pine nuts. Toss well, then taste and adjust the seasoning if necessary. Spoon into pasta bowls and drizzle with oil if desired. Serve with more grated cheese.

Penne WITH VODKA SAUCE

Aside from the fresh basil—and even that grows abundantly on my patio during the summer—every ingredient for this dish is always on hand in my pantry or refrigerator. The vodka sauce, a bright tomato sauce enriched with heavy cream, comes together in the time it takes to boil the pasta. You won't really taste the vodka; it's simply there to cut the richness of the dish.

Serves 4 to 6

3 tablespoons unsalted butter

¾ cup (105 g) finely chopped yellow onion (from 1 small onion)

3 garlic cloves, minced

½ teaspoon red pepper flakes

1 (28-ounce/794 g) can whole peeled plum tomatoes, chopped, with their juices (see Pro Tip, page 57)

2 tablespoons tomato paste

1 teaspoon salt

½ teaspoon sugar

⅓ cup (80 mL) vodka

1 pound (454 g) penne pasta

⅔ cup (160 mL) heavy cream

3 tablespoons chopped fresh basil, plus more for serving

Finely grated Parmigiano-Reggiano cheese, for serving

1. Bring a large pot of salted water to a boil.

2. Heat the butter in a 3-quart (3 L) saucepan over medium heat until shimmering. Add the onion and cook, stirring frequently, until softened and translucent, 3 to 4 minutes. Add the garlic and red pepper flakes and cook, stirring constantly, for 30 seconds more. Do not brown. Add the tomatoes and their juices, tomato paste, salt, sugar, and vodka; bring to a boil. Reduce the heat to medium low and cook at a lively simmer, uncovered, stirring occasionally, for 10 minutes.

3. While the sauce simmers, boil the pasta according to the package instructions until just shy of al dente. Before draining, ladle out about 1 cup (240 mL) of the pasta cooking water and set it aside. Drain the pasta, then return it to the pot.

4. Stir the cream into the sauce and simmer, uncovered, for about 3 minutes more. Using an immersion blender, puree the sauce until mostly smooth, leaving some small chunks. (Alternatively, ladle some of the sauce into a blender and puree. Be sure to remove the center knob on the blender and cover with a dish towel to avoid splatters, then pour back into the pan.)

5. Pour the sauce over the penne. It may seem a little soupy; that's okay. Bring the sauce and pasta to a gentle boil over medium-high heat, stirring frequently; cook until the sauce is reduced and thickened enough to cling to the pasta, a few minutes. Add a little of the reserved pasta water if the pasta seems dry. Stir in the basil, then taste and adjust seasoning if necessary. Serve, passing the grated Parmigiano-Reggiano at the table.

PRO TIPS

When combining a sauce with cooked pasta, always cook the two together in the pot for a minute or two before serving. This marries the flavors and helps the sauce cling to the pasta.

—

If you'd like to add a little something special to this dish, try crisping a few thin slices of prosciutto and crumbling them over each serving. Simply place a few slices of prosciutto between 2 paper towels on a microwave-safe plate. Microwave on high for 1 minute. Remove the paper towel covering the prosciutto and let the prosciutto sit for a few seconds until crisp. Crispy prosciutto is also delicious crumbled over salads and soups.

Risotto WITH ASPARAGUS & PEAS

SOURCING SAVVY

Arborio rice is a short-grained, high-starch Italian rice that becomes creamy and slightly chewy when cooked. You can find it in the rice section of most supermarkets.

Comforting to eat—and comforting to make (all that stirring is like mindful meditation!)—risotto is a Northern Italian rice dish cooked gently until it reaches a creamy consistency. Most people think of it as a restaurant-style dish, but it's easy to make at home with very few ingredients. There's lots of room for creativity here. Don't feel like asparagus? Substitute zucchini or mushrooms. Going vegetarian? Replace the chicken broth with vegetable broth. Want to zhoosh it up? Stir in some fresh herbs at the end. You really can't go wrong!

Serves 4

6 cups (1.4 L) low-sodium chicken broth

4 tablespoons (½ stick/2 ounces/ 56 g) unsalted butter

1 bunch of asparagus, preferably thin, trimmed and cut into 1-inch (2.5 cm) pieces

¼ teaspoon salt

Freshly ground black pepper

1 cup (120 g) frozen peas

1 medium yellow onion, finely chopped

2 garlic cloves, minced

1½ cups (300 g) Arborio rice

½ cup (120 mL) dry white wine

½ cup (50 g) grated Parmigiano-Reggiano cheese, plus more for serving

1. In a medium pot, bring the broth to a simmer.

2. Meanwhile, in a large pot or Dutch oven, melt 1 tablespoon of the butter over medium-low heat. Add the asparagus, salt, and a few grinds of pepper. Cook, stirring frequently, until the asparagus is crisp-tender, 2 to 4 minutes. Add the peas and continue cooking until the peas are thawed, about 1 minute. Transfer the vegetables to a plate.

3. In the same pot (no need to clean) over medium-low heat, melt 2 table-spoons of the butter. Add the onion and cook, stirring frequently, until translucent, 2 to 3 minutes. Add the garlic and cook for 1 minute more. Do not brown. Add the rice and cook, stirring constantly, until glossy and translucent around the edges, about 2 minutes. Add the wine and cook until completely absorbed, about 1 minute. Ladle about 1 cup (240 mL) of the simmering broth into the rice and cook, stirring occasionally, until absorbed. Continue adding the broth, 1 cup (240 mL) at a time and stirring frequently, until it is absorbed and the rice is al dente and creamy, about 25 minutes. (Be careful not to get distracted while the rice is cooking; although it doesn't require a lot of skill, it does require you to keep a close eye on it to prevent sticking.)

4. Stir the reserved vegetables, the Parmigiano-Reggiano, and the remaining tablespoon of butter into the risotto. Taste and adjust the seasoning with salt and pepper if necessary. If the risotto is too thick, thin it with a bit of milk. Serve, passing the grated Parmigiano-Reggiano at the table.

Linguine
WITH SHELLFISH, TOMATOES & SAFFRON

I love to serve this dish on our back patio in the summer. If I close my eyes, I can almost pretend I'm sitting al fresco at a seaside Italian restaurant. There's just something about shellfish and pasta in a briny, saffron-infused sauce that evokes sun and sea for me. Make sure to have all your ingredients prepped in advance; once you start cooking, this dish comes together quickly.

Serves 4

1 pound (454 g) linguine pasta

¼ cup (60 mL) extra-virgin olive oil

½ cup (60 g) finely chopped shallot (from 1 large shallot)

6 garlic cloves, coarsely chopped

1 cup (240 mL) dry white wine

Generous pinch of saffron threads, crushed (about ⅛ teaspoon)

½ teaspoon red pepper flakes

1 (14.5-ounce/411 g) can crushed tomatoes

2 tablespoons tomato paste

2 teaspoons anchovy paste (see Sourcing Savvy)

1 teaspoon salt

2 pounds (907 g) mussels, scrubbed and debearded (see How to Store and Clean Mussels Prior to Cooking, page 98)

¾ pound (340 g) large (31/35) shrimp, peeled and deveined

3 tablespoons unsalted butter, cut into 3 pieces

¼ cup (10 g) chopped fresh Italian parsley

SOURCING SAVVY

You may experience a bit of sticker shock if you've never purchased saffron; it is harvested by hand, making it the most expensive spice in the world. Fortunately, it is generally sold in small quantities, and you usually only need a pinch. Saffron threads should be crushed to release their flavor before they are added to recipes. Simply use your thumb and forefinger to crush the threads into fine pieces. Be sure to use only the amount that the recipe calls for; too much can give food a medicinal taste. Store any leftover saffron for up to 6 months wrapped in foil and placed in an airtight container in a cool, dark place.

Made from ground anchovy fillets, anchovy paste adds delicious umami flavor to recipes without having to deal with actual anchovies. It comes in a tube and will keep for months in the refrigerator. (It's delicious in Caesar salad dressing.)

1. Bring a large pot of salted water to a boil. Add the linguine and cook according to the package directions until about 1 minute shy of al dente (the pasta should still be quite firm to the bite, since it will cook another minute or two in the sauce).

2. Meanwhile, in a Dutch oven or large pot with a tight-fitting lid, heat the oil over medium heat until shimmering. Add the shallot and cook, stirring constantly, until softened, about 2 minutes. Add the garlic and cook, stirring constantly, for about 1 minute more; do not brown. Add the wine, saffron, red pepper flakes, crushed tomatoes, tomato paste, anchovy paste, and salt; stir to combine.

3. Add the mussels to the pot and bring the sauce to a boil. Reduce the heat to medium-low and cook, covered, until the mussels open, 5 to 8 minutes. Using tongs or a slotted spoon, remove the mussels from the pan and place them in a large bowl (discard any unopened mussels). Cover the bowl with foil to keep warm.

-RECIPE CONTINUES-

4. Add the shrimp to the pot and bring to a simmer; cook, covered, until the shrimp are opaque, 2 to 3 minutes. Using a slotted spoon, transfer the shrimp to the bowl with the mussels and cover to keep warm.

5. Reserving 1 cup (240 mL) of the pasta cooking water, drain the linguine in a colander (do not rinse). Add the pasta to the pot with the sauce. Increase the heat to medium and cook, tossing occasionally, until the pasta absorbs most of the sauce and is just tender, 1 to 2 minutes. Add the reserved cooking water if needed to provide more moisture.

6. Remove the pan from the heat. Add the butter and parsley and toss to coat. Taste and adjust the seasoning if necessary. Return the mussels and shrimp to the pot; toss with tongs until evenly combined. Serve with bowls for the mussel shells.

HOW TO STORE AND CLEAN MUSSELS PRIOR TO COOKING

When you purchase mussels, they're still alive. After bringing them home from the store, they will stay fresh in the refrigerator for 1 to 2 days. Because they're alive, avoid storing them in a plastic bag or airtight container. Instead, place them in a bowl, covered with a damp cloth or wet paper towel.

When you're ready to cook the mussels, place them in a colander and run them under cold running water. Use your hands or a scrubbing brush to remove any sand or remaining debris. If beards (the little tufts of fibers mussels use to connect to rocks or pilings) are present, cut or scrape them off with a paring knife, or use your fingers to pull them sharply down toward the hinged point of the shells. The mussels should be tightly closed. If you see one that is open, tap it gently against the counter; in a live mussel, this will trigger a reaction to close its shell. If the mussel doesn't slowly close, it has died and should be discarded. Discard any mussels with cracked shells as well.

Drunken-Style Noodles

WITH SHRIMP

This recipe is inspired by the popular Thai street food dish pad kee mao, or "drunken noodles." Contrary to what the name implies, the dish does not contain alcohol. Pad means "stir fry" and kee mao means "drunkard," so it's not the noodles that are drunk but, rather, the person who is eating them! I'm sure the dish is comforting after a night of partying—or that it's spicy enough to sober you up—but for me it's simply a delicious weeknight dinner, ice-cold beer optional. I call this version "drunken-style" because, traditionally, drunken noodles are made with fresh wide rice noodles. I use medium rice noodles because I can count on them being stocked in my grocery store—these are the noodles used for pad Thai, which makes the recipe more of a drunken noodle–pad Thai hybrid.

For maximum efficiency, use the time during which the noodles soak to prepare the other ingredients. Also, you'll need several bowls for the ingredients. Make cleanup a bit quicker by using your "everyday" bowls for the eggs and the sauce; that way, you can just pop them in the dishwasher instead of hand-washing them.

Serves 4

8 cups (2 L) plus ¾ cup (177 mL) water, plus more as needed

8 ounces (227 g) rice noodles, as thick as you can find

2 tablespoons oyster sauce

2 tablespoons soy sauce

1½ tablespoons fish sauce

1½ tablespoons sriracha, or to taste

1 tablespoon dark brown sugar

3 large eggs

Salt

5 tablespoons (75 mL) vegetable oil

1 pound (454 g) large (31/35) shrimp, peeled and deveined

2½ cups (190 g) bite-sized broccoli florets (from an 8-ounce/225 g broccoli crown)

1 bunch of scallions (light and dark green parts separated), thinly sliced

4 garlic cloves, minced

½ cup (8 g) loosely packed Thai or Italian basil leaves, roughly chopped

1 tablespoon fresh lime juice (from 1 lime)

Lime wedges, for serving (optional)

SOURCING SAVVY
Oyster sauce is a thick, dark brown condiment made primarily from oyster extracts. Despite its name, oyster sauce doesn't taste strongly of oysters; rather, it has a salty, savory, slightly sweet flavor. You can find it in most supermarkets.

1. Soak the noodles: Bring the 8 cups (2 L) water to a boil in a large pot. Remove the pot from the heat and add the rice noodles. Stir very well so they don't stick, then let soak, stirring frequently, until soft, pliable, and just shy of perfectly cooked (they should be al dente, just like regular pasta). This process should take 10 to 20 minutes; check the noodles frequently as the soaking

-RECIPE CONTINUES-

time varies greatly depending on the width and brand of the noodles. Drain and rinse well with cold water. (If not using the noodles right away, toss them with a little oil to prevent sticking.)

2. In a medium bowl, whisk together the oyster sauce, soy sauce, fish sauce, sriracha, brown sugar, and ¼ cup (60 mL) of the water.

3. In a small bowl, beat the eggs with ⅛ teaspoon salt.

4. Heat 1 tablespoon of the oil in a large (12-inch/30 cm) nonstick skillet over medium-high heat until shimmering. Add the shrimp and sprinkle with ⅛ teaspoon salt; cook, tossing occasionally, until the shrimp are opaque and just cooked through, about 2 minutes. Transfer the shrimp to a large bowl.

5. Add 1 tablespoon of the oil to the skillet; add the eggs and scramble until cooked through. Transfer the eggs to the bowl with the shrimp.

6. Add the broccoli to the pan along with ⅛ teaspoon salt and the remaining ½ cup (120 mL) water. Cover and steam until cooked through, about 2 minutes. Using a slotted spoon, transfer the broccoli to the bowl with the shrimp and eggs. Discard any excess water from the pan and wipe it clean with a moist paper towel.

7. Return the pan to the stove, increase the heat to high, and add the remaining 3 tablespoons oil. When the oil is shimmering, add the light scallions and garlic and cook, stirring constantly, until fragrant, about 1 minute.

8. Add the noodles and sauce to the pan and toss with tongs until the noodles absorb the sauce and are perfectly tender, 3 to 5 minutes. If the noodles remain a bit tough at this point, add 2 tablespoons water to the skillet and continue to toss and cook until tender. Repeat with more water as necessary.

9. Add the shrimp, eggs, and broccoli, the dark scallions, and the basil and lime juice to the skillet and toss until heated through. Taste and adjust seasoning if necessary. If the noodles seem dry, add another tablespoon or so of water. Serve immediately with lime wedges, if desired.

Fettuccine Carbonara
WITH PEAS

Carbonara is a traditional Italian pasta dish made with egg, grated cheese, cured pork, and lots of black pepper. This version isn't quite authentic—I don't think you'll find a single Italian chef who puts shallots or peas in their carbonara—but it's a cozy all-in-one supper that you can whip up in 20 minutes, and you know anything with crispy bacon is bound to please.

Serves 4

2 large eggs

2 large egg yolks

¾ cup (75 g) finely grated Parmigiano-Reggiano cheese

Heaping ½ teaspoon salt

¾ teaspoon freshly ground black pepper

½ pound (227 g) thick-cut bacon (about 6 slices), diced

½ cup (60 g) minced shallot (from 1 large shallot)

3 garlic cloves, minced

1 cup (120 g) frozen peas, thawed

1 pound (454 g) fettuccine, preferably fresh (from the refrigerated case)

HEADS UP

When making carbonara, it's important that the pasta is very hot when combining it with the sauce, as the heat from the pasta finishes cooking the raw eggs. However, this should be done off the heat because if the pan is too hot, the eggs will scramble.

1. Bring a large pot of salted water to a boil.

2. Meanwhile, in a medium bowl, whisk together the eggs, egg yolks, Parmigiano-Reggiano, salt, and pepper.

3. In a medium skillet over medium-high heat, cook the bacon, stirring frequently, until crispy, 7 to 9 minutes. Turn off the heat, and using a slotted spoon, transfer the bacon to a paper towel–lined plate to drain. Pour off and discard all but about 2 tablespoons of the bacon fat. Let the pan cool for a minute or so and then set over low heat. Add the shallot and cook until softened, a few minutes. Add the garlic and cook 1 minute more. Add the peas and cook until just warmed through, about 1 minute. Remove from the heat.

4. Cook the fettuccine according to the package instructions for al dente. Reserve 1 cup (240 mL) of the pasta cooking water, then drain and return the fettuccine to the pot.

5. Whisking constantly, add ⅔ cup (160 mL) of the hot reserved pasta water to the egg/cheese mixture (whisking vigorously will prevent the egg from curdling).

6. Add the pea mixture to the hot fettuccine and set the pot over medium heat. Using tongs, toss for 1 to 2 minutes, or until evenly combined and hot. Off the heat, immediately pour the egg mixture over the pasta and peas and toss to combine (it may seem too wet at first, but the sauce will continue to thicken as you toss). Stir in the bacon, then taste and adjust the seasoning as necessary. If the pasta seems dry, add the remaining pasta cooking water, little by little, until creamy. If it seems too liquidy, set the pot over very low heat and toss constantly until the sauce is thickened. Serve immediately.

Baked Ziti WITH SAUSAGE

This dish is a major family-pleaser. Loaded with Italian sausage, which packs a ton of flavor, it's similar to lasagna but without the fuss; it's easy enough for a weeknight but also special enough for company; and it makes a great prep-ahead potluck dish. To save time, go ahead and use pre-shredded mozzarella cheese from a bag; just be sure it's made from whole milk (low-fat won't taste nearly as good).

Serves 8 to 10

1 pound (454 g) ziti noodles

1½ pounds (680 g) spicy or sweet bulk Italian sausage (or removed from casings)

4 garlic cloves, minced

1 (28-ounce/794 g) can crushed tomatoes

1 teaspoon salt

1½ teaspoons sugar

¼ teaspoon red pepper flakes

1 cup (240 mL) heavy cream

½ cup (50 g) finely grated pecorino Romano or Parmigiano-Reggiano cheese

⅓ cup (13 g) chopped fresh basil (optional)

2 cups (227 g) shredded whole-milk mozzarella cheese

1. Bring a large pot of salted water to a boil. Cook the ziti according to the package directions for very al dente, about 7 minutes. (It will continue to cook in the oven, so you want to undercook it just a bit.) Drain and put the pasta back into the pot.

2. Preheat the oven to 425°F (220°C) and set the oven rack in the middle position.

3. Heat a large nonstick sauté pan over medium-high heat. Crumble the sausage into the pan and cook, breaking it apart with a wooden spoon, until lightly browned and just cooked through, 5 to 6 minutes. Use a slotted spoon to transfer the cooked sausage to a plate. Drain all but 1 tablespoon of the fat from the pan and set over low heat (if you don't have enough fat in the pan, add a tablespoon of olive oil). Add the garlic and cook, stirring constantly with a wooden spoon, until soft but not browned, about 1 minute. Add the crushed tomatoes, salt, sugar, and red pepper flakes and simmer, uncovered, for 10 minutes.

4. Add the cream, ⅓ cup (33 g) of the pecorino Romano, the cooked sausage, and the basil, if using, to the pan; stir until evenly combined. Carefully pour the contents of the sauté pan into the pot with the pasta and gently stir to combine. Spoon half the mixture into a 9 x 13-inch (23 x 33 cm) baking dish. Sprinkle with half the shredded mozzarella and half the remaining pecorino Romano. Spoon the remaining pasta mixture on top and sprinkle with the remaining mozzarella and pecorino Romano.

5. Transfer to the oven and bake, uncovered, until the cheese has melted and browned, 15 to 20 minutes. Serve immediately.

Kids-Love-It Beefy Chili Mac

A regular menu item in the school cafeteria when I was growing up, chili mac is one of those nostalgic dishes that reminds me of my childhood. It's a comforting one-pot dish that you can have on the table in less than 45 minutes. When my kids were younger, it was one of my go-to weeknight dinners. Now I make a big batch when my nephews, Max and Leo (ages 7 and 5), come for dinner. I mean, with pasta, cheese, and ground beef, how can you go wrong with kids? Serve it with tortilla chips for dipping or crushing over the top.

Serves 4

2 tablespoons vegetable oil

1 large yellow onion, finely chopped

4 garlic cloves, finely chopped

1 tablespoon ancho chile powder

1 tablespoon ground cumin

1½ teaspoons smoked paprika

¼ teaspoon cayenne pepper (optional)

1½ teaspoons salt

1 pound (454 g) 85% or 90% lean ground beef

3 cups (710 mL) chicken broth

1 (8-ounce/227 g) can tomato sauce

1 teaspoon dried oregano

1 teaspoon sugar

8 ounces (about 2 cups/227 g) elbow macaroni

1 cup (240 mL) evaporated milk

1½ cups (170 g) shredded Mexican cheese blend, plus more for serving

3 scallions (dark green parts only), thinly sliced

Tortilla chips, for serving

1. Heat the oil in a large pot or Dutch oven over medium heat until shimmering. Add the onion and cook, stirring occasionally, until softened, 3 to 4 minutes. Add the garlic, chile powder, cumin, smoked paprika, cayenne (if using), and salt and cook, stirring often, about 1 minute more. Add the ground beef and cook, stirring and breaking it apart, until no longer pink, 3 to 5 minutes.

2. Stir in the broth, tomato sauce, oregano, sugar, and macaroni and bring to a boil. Reduce the heat to low, cover, and simmer, stirring every so often so the macaroni doesn't stick to the bottom, until the pasta is al dente, 9 to 12 minutes. Use a soup spoon to skim any grease off the top if necessary.

3. Off the heat, add the evaporated milk and the cheese and stir until the cheese is melted. Taste and adjust the seasoning if necessary. Ladle the chili mac into bowls and sprinkle with the scallions. Serve with more shredded cheese and tortilla chips.

Marvelous Meatballs

Lamb Kofta

WITH TZATZIKI

MAKE-AHEAD/FREEZER-FRIENDLY INSTRUCTIONS

The patties can be formed and refrigerated for up to 2 days, or frozen for up to 3 months. (Freeze the patties on a baking sheet or plate so their shape sets, then transfer them to a resealable freezer bag for easy storage.) If frozen, defrost overnight in the refrigerator and then cook as directed.

Kofta is a Middle Eastern dish made from ground lamb or beef mixed with onions, garlic, and spices. The meat mixture is shaped into balls, patties, or logs and then grilled and served with pita, salads, dips, and sauces. There are endless variations of kofta throughout the Middle East—I have a fantastic recipe for Persian beef kofta in my first cookbook—but I learned this version from a kebab maker in the Old City of Jerusalem, when we were there a few years ago celebrating our kids' b'nai mitzvah. His secret was adding minced vegetables, toasted nuts, herbs, and spices to the meat to give the kofta a deep, complex flavor. • PHOTOGRAPH ON PAGE 108

Serves 6 (Makes about 28 patties)

¼ cup (30 g) pine nuts

¼ cup (30 g) almonds

¼ cup (30 g) walnuts

1 small yellow onion, roughly chopped

3 garlic cloves, roughly chopped

1 small red bell pepper, roughly chopped

1 small jalapeño pepper, seeds and ribs removed, roughly chopped (see Pro Tip)

½ cup (8 g) gently packed cilantro leaves

2 pounds (907 g) ground lamb

¾ teaspoon ground cumin

Heaping ¼ teaspoon ground cinnamon

Heaping ¼ teaspoon ground cardamom

Heaping ¼ teaspoon ground cloves

1½ teaspoons salt

¼ teaspoon white pepper

Tzatziki, homemade (recipe follows) or store-bought, for serving

1. Place all the nuts in the bowl of a food processor and pulse until finely chopped but not pasty. Transfer the nuts to a small dry skillet over medium heat; cook, stirring frequently, until lightly browned and fragrant, 5 to 6 minutes. Pour the nuts into a mixing bowl large enough to hold all the ingredients and set aside to cool. (Don't leave the nuts in the pan, as the residual heat may cause them to burn.)

2. Place the onion, garlic, bell pepper, jalapeño, and cilantro in the bowl of the food processor (no need to clean it first). Pulse until the vegetables are finely minced but not pureed. Set a fine-mesh sieve over a medium bowl. Transfer the minced vegetables to the sieve and use a rubber spatula to press out as much liquid as possible. Add the strained vegetable mixture to the bowl with the nuts.

3. To the veggies and toasted nuts, add the ground lamb, cumin, cinnamon, cardamom, cloves, salt, and white pepper. Using your hands, work the mixture together until evenly combined.

4. Line a baking sheet with aluminum foil. Form the mixture into patties about 2 inches (5 cm) in diameter and ½ inch (13 mm) thick. Place on the baking sheet, cover with plastic wrap, and refrigerate while you preheat the grill, or until ready to cook.

5. Preheat a grill to medium-high heat. Using tongs, dip a wad of paper towels in vegetable oil and carefully wipe the grill grate several times until glossy and coated. Place the kofta on the grill and cook, covered, until browned and cooked through, about 4 minutes per side. Serve with tzatziki.

Tzatziki

This refreshing and good-for-you yogurt and cucumber dip is wonderful with the kofta meatballs and stuffed into pita bread. It's also excellent alongside grilled meats or vegetables.

Makes 2 cups

1½ cups (360 g) plain 2% Greek yogurt (I use Fage)

1 medium English/hothouse cucumber, seeded, coarsely grated, and squeezed as dry as possible

2 small garlic cloves, minced

2 tablespoons extra-virgin olive oil, plus more for serving

Scant ¾ teaspoon salt

¼ teaspoon freshly ground black pepper

2 tablespoons finely chopped fresh mint, plus more for serving

Combine all the ingredients in a medium bowl and mix until blended. Taste and adjust the seasoning if necessary. Cover and chill until ready to serve. Before serving, drizzle with a bit of oil and sprinkle with fresh mint if desired.

I like the depth of flavor that the 3 varieties of nuts provide, but if you have only 1 or 2 kinds, that's okay; just make sure you use a total of ¾ cup (90 g).

If you like your kofta spicy, reserve some of the seeds from the jalapeño and add them with the vegetables. Be sure to wash your hands well after handling hot peppers, and never touch your eyes while working with them.

Turkey, Spinach & Cheese Meatballs

I used to be one of those opinionated people who felt you shouldn't sneak vegetables into your children's food, but then I gave birth to a picky eater and all that righteousness went right out the window. Parenting is nothing if not humbling, right? These meatballs are a great way to sneak in some spinach, but what makes them really special is the addition of turkey sausage. Not only does the sausage make the meatballs tender, but it also adds great flavor without the need for a ton of other ingredients.

Serves 6 (makes about 30 meatballs)

1 tablespoon extra-virgin olive oil

1 large egg

3½ cups (85 g) baby spinach leaves, chopped

3 scallions (light and dark green parts), thinly sliced

3 garlic cloves, minced

1¼ pounds (567 g) 93% lean ground turkey (preferably Shady Brook Farms)

1¼ pounds (567 g) Italian turkey sausage, removed from the casings (preferably Shady Brook Farms)

1 cup (120 g) shredded whole-milk mozzarella cheese

⅓ cup (33 g) finely grated Parmigiano-Reggiano cheese, plus more for serving

½ cup (70 g) Italian-seasoned bread crumbs

1 (24-ounce/680 g) jar good-quality marinara sauce, or homemade marinara

1. Preheat the broiler and set an oven rack on the second-highest level. Line a baking sheet with heavy-duty aluminum foil and grease it with the oil.

2. In a bowl large enough to hold all the ingredients, beat the egg. Add the spinach, scallions, and garlic and stir until evenly combined. Add the ground turkey, turkey sausage, mozzarella, Parmigiano-Reggiano, and bread crumbs. Using your hands, mix until evenly combined. Shape the mixture into 1½-inch (4 cm) balls and place them on the prepared baking sheet.

3. Broil the meatballs until golden brown on top, about 10 minutes.

4. Meanwhile, heat the marinara sauce over medium heat in a large saucepan on the stovetop. Add the broiled meatballs and simmer, covered, over low heat for 5 to 10 minutes, or until the meatballs are fully cooked.

Sheet Pan Chicken & Pancetta Meatballs

WITH TOMATO BALSAMIC GLAZE

Inspired by an old *Gourmet* magazine recipe, these meatballs are an upgraded version of the popular chicken meatballs on my website. They are packed with flavor, thanks to a good bit of crispy pancetta and pecorino Romano cheese. The tangy-sweet glaze adds a nice pop of flavor and dresses up the meatballs. Pair them with a salad and Rustic Parmesan Mashed Potatoes (page 171).

Serves 4 (Makes about 12 meatballs)

FOR THE MEATBALLS

4 ounces (113 g) finely diced pancetta

1 large egg

2 tablespoons chopped fresh basil

1 tablespoon tomato paste

1 garlic clove, minced

¼ cup (60 mL) milk

Scant ¼ teaspoon salt

½ teaspoon freshly ground black pepper

1 pound (454 g) ground chicken (avoid extra-lean 100% breast meat)

½ cup (50 g) finely grated pecorino Romano cheese

6 tablespoons (53g) Italian-seasoned bread crumbs

FOR THE GLAZE

2 tablespoons tomato paste

2 tablespoons extra-virgin olive oil

2½ teaspoons balsamic vinegar

1 teaspoon sugar

MAKE AHEAD/FREEZER-FRIENDLY INSTRUCTIONS

The cooked meatballs can be made up to 2 days ahead and refrigerated, or frozen for up to 3 months. If frozen, defrost overnight in the refrigerator and then reheat, tightly covered with foil, in a 300°F (150°C) oven until hot in the center.

PRO TIP

Be sure the pancetta is finely diced; you don't want big chunks in the meatballs. I buy the 4-ounce (113 g) package of mini-cubed pancetta from Trader Joe's. If you'd like to make the meatballs without the pancetta, as in my original website version, double the salt in the recipe.

1. Preheat the oven to 350°F (175°C). Line a 13 x 18-inch (33 x 46 cm) baking sheet with parchment paper.

2. Make the meatballs: In a small nonstick pan over medium heat, cook the pancetta until crispy and the fat is rendered, 7 to 9 minutes. Using a slotted spoon, transfer the pancetta to a paper towel–lined plate and let cool.

3. Meanwhile, in a large bowl, combine the egg, basil, tomato paste, garlic, milk, salt, and pepper. Mix well with a wire whisk, making sure the tomato paste is completely dissolved.

4. Add the ground chicken, grated cheese, bread crumbs, and the pancetta. Use a fork to mash the ingredients together until evenly combined; the mixture will be somewhat wet. Moisten your hands to prevent sticking, then form 12 medium balls (slightly larger than a golf ball) and place them on the prepared baking sheet.

5. Make the glaze: Combine the tomato paste, oil, vinegar, and sugar in a small bowl and whisk until smooth. Brush the glaze evenly over the meatballs. Bake for 25 to 30 minutes, until the meatballs are cooked through, and serve.

Vietnamese-Style Meatballs
WITH CHILI SAUCE, FRESH HERBS & PEANUTS

MAKE-AHEAD/FREEZER-FRIENDLY INSTRUCTIONS

The meatballs can be fully prepared 2 days ahead and refrigerated, or frozen for up to 3 months. If frozen, defrost overnight in the refrigerator and then reheat in the microwave.

SOURCING SAVVY

Sambal Oelek is an Indonesian chili paste made from a variety of chile peppers, vinegar, and salt. It's a nice addition to stir-fries and marinades, or as a condiment for Asian noodle dishes. It can be found in most supermarkets. Asian chili-garlic sauce is similar to Sambal Oelek, but with the addition of garlic, and can be substituted.

These tender beef and pork meatballs with a deliciously bright and pungent sauce are one of the most popular recipes on my website. They are flavored with fish sauce and soy sauce—two umami-rich condiments—along with ginger, lime, Sambal Oelek (not a traditional Vietnamese ingredient, but the spicy, garlicky flavor works so well here), and fresh herbs. They practically explode with flavor. I love them over rice, but they are also delicious wrapped in lettuce cups or served over rice noodles. Be judicious with the chili sauce—a little goes a long way.

Serves 4 to 6 (Makes about 22 meatballs)

FOR THE MEATBALLS

2 large eggs

3 tablespoons fish sauce

2 garlic cloves, minced

1 tablespoon finely grated fresh ginger (from a peeled 1-inch/2.5 cm knob)

¼ teaspoon red pepper flakes

3 scallions (light and dark green parts), thinly sliced, plus extra for serving

2 teaspoons grated lime zest (from 2 limes)

3 tablespoons chopped fresh cilantro, plus more for serving

3 tablespoons chopped fresh mint, plus more for serving

¾ pound (340 g) 85% lean ground beef

¾ pound (340 g) ground pork

1 cup (60 g) panko bread crumbs

½ cup (70 g) chopped unsalted peanuts, for serving

FOR THE SAUCE

¼ cup (120 mL) fresh lime juice (from 2 to 3 limes)

¼ cup (120 mL) soy sauce

2 tablespoons fish sauce

2 tablespoons Sambal Oelek or Asian-style chili-garlic sauce

¼ cup (50 g) sugar

1. Preheat the oven to 400°F (205°C) and set an oven rack in the middle position.

2. Make the meatballs: In a large bowl, whisk together the eggs, fish sauce, garlic, ginger, red pepper flakes, scallions, lime zest, cilantro, and mint. Add the ground beef, ground pork, and panko. Using your hands, mix until evenly combined. Roll the mixture into golf ball–size meatballs and arrange on an unlined baking sheet. The mixture will be a bit sticky; dampen your hands every so often while rolling the meatballs, if necessary.

3. Bake for 25 minutes, flipping once with a metal spatula halfway through the cooking time, until the meatballs are browned and cooked through. (If the meatballs stick a bit to the pan, simply slide the metal spatula underneath them and they should release.)

4. Make the sauce: Meanwhile, whisk together the lime juice, soy sauce, fish sauce, Sambal Oelek, and sugar in a medium bowl. Be sure the sugar is completely dissolved and not stuck to the bottom of the bowl. Taste and add more chili sauce if desired.

5. Serve the meatballs drizzled with the sauce and sprinkled with additional scallions, cilantro, mint, and the peanuts.

Saucy Sesame-Ginger Meatballs

Served over steaming white rice, these meatballs in a sweet sesame sauce make a quick, kid-friendly supper. The sauce has a little kick to balance out the sweetness, but it's not spicy. In keeping with the kid-friendly theme, I serve these meatballs with edamame seasoned with a pinch of salt.

Serves 4 to 6 (Makes about 22 meatballs)

FOR THE MEATBALLS

Nonstick cooking spray

1 large egg

1 tablespoon soy sauce

3 tablespoons water

¼ cup (12 g) thinly sliced scallions (light and dark green parts), plus more for serving (from 1 bunch)

2 garlic cloves, minced

2 teaspoons grated fresh ginger (from a 1-inch/2.5 cm knob)

1½ pounds (680 g) meatloaf mix (see Sourcing Savvy)

⅔ cup (93 g) plain bread crumbs

FOR THE SAUCE

1 cup (260 g) ketchup

½ cup (80 mL) water

6 tablespoons (87 g) packed dark brown sugar

2 tablespoons soy sauce

1½ tablespoons Sambal Oelek or Asian chili-garlic sauce (see Sourcing Savvy, page 116)

1 teaspoon toasted sesame oil

1 tablespoon rice vinegar

FOR SERVING

Cooked white rice

1 tablespoon sesame seeds

MAKE-AHEAD/FREEZER-FRIENDLY INSTRUCTIONS

The dish can be fully prepared and refrigerated up to 2 days ahead of time, or frozen for up to 3 months. If frozen, defrost overnight in the refrigerator; when ready to serve, reheat on the stovetop over medium heat until the meatballs and sauce are warmed through.

SOURCING SAVVY

Most grocery stores sell "meatloaf mix," a combination of ground beef, pork, and veal that is ideal for making meatloaf and meatballs. If you can't find it, use equal parts ground beef and pork.

1. Make the meatballs: Preheat the oven to 400°F (205°C) and set an oven rack in the middle position. Line a baking sheet with heavy-duty aluminum foil and spray with nonstick cooking spray.

2. In a large bowl, whisk together the egg, soy sauce, water, scallions, garlic, and ginger. Add the meatloaf mix and bread crumbs and, using your hands, work the mixture until evenly combined. Roll into golf ball–size meatballs and place them on the prepared baking sheet. Bake until lightly browned and just cooked, flipping halfway through, 18 to 20 minutes.

3. Make the sauce: Meanwhile, in a large skillet, stir together the ketchup, water, brown sugar, soy sauce, Sambal Oelek, sesame oil, and rice vinegar.

4. Bring the sauce to a simmer over medium heat. Using tongs, place the meatballs in the sauce and cook, uncovered, stirring the meatballs occasionally, for about 5 minutes, or until the sauce is slightly thickened and the meatballs are nicely coated. Spoon the meatballs over rice and sprinkle with the additional scallions and the sesame seeds.

Chicken Winners

Moroccan-Spiced Grilled Chicken

WITH WARM COUSCOUS SALAD & APRICOT VINAIGRETTE

Allow at least 5 hours to marinate the chicken.

MAKE-AHEAD INSTRUCTIONS

The couscous salad can be prepared and refrigerated in an airtight container up to 2 days ahead of time. Bring it to room temperature before serving.

PRO TIP

Because chicken breasts are so lean, many cooks marinate them before grilling to ensure they are juicy and plump. However, it's often the marinade that causes chicken to become dry! Contrary to popular belief, acidic ingredients like wine vinegar or lemon juice do not tenderize lean chicken breasts. Just the opposite: they "cook" the exterior of the meat and give it a leathery texture. When it comes to boneless, skinless chicken breasts, be generous with the oil, garlic, and seasoning but skip the citrus and vinegar. You'll notice a big difference!

I love Moroccan food, especially how dishes often combine spicy, savory, and sweet flavors, and that's the idea behind this easy and elegant dinner. The spices in the chicken marinade are reminiscent of ras el hanout, a North African spice blend that usually contains more than a dozen spices, like cumin, coriander, ginger, turmeric, cinnamon, cayenne pepper, cardamom, allspice, fenugreek, and more. You could serve the couscous plain (see page 172)—admittedly, my kids prefer it that way—but it takes only a few extra minutes to jazz it up, and the sweet and tangy apricot vinaigrette pairs beautifully with the warm spices on the chicken. • PHOTOGRAPH ON PAGE 120

Serves 4

FOR THE CHICKEN

1¾ pounds (794 g) boneless, skinless chicken breasts or chicken tenders

¼ cup (60 mL) extra-virgin olive oil

1 teaspoon salt

1 teaspoon sugar

3 garlic cloves, minced

2 teaspoons paprika

1 teaspoon ground cumin

½ teaspoon ground coriander

¼ teaspoon ground ginger

¼ teaspoon ground turmeric

¼ teaspoon ground cinnamon

⅛ teaspoon cayenne pepper

FOR THE COUSCOUS SALAD

1½ cups (360 mL) low-sodium chicken broth

1 tablespoon unsalted butter

½ teaspoon salt

1½ cups (10 ounces/283 g) couscous

¼ cup plus 2 tablespoons (120 g) apricot jam

4½ tablespoons (68 mL) extra-virgin olive oil

3 tablespoons white wine vinegar

Freshly ground black pepper

2 scallions (light and green parts), thinly sliced

2 tablespoons chopped fresh parsley or mint (optional)

⅓ cup (33 g) sliced almonds

1. Make the chicken: Place a chicken breast in a resealable freezer bag and use a meat mallet or rolling pin to pound it to an even ½-inch (13 mm) thickness. Remove from the bag and set aside. Repeat with the remaining breasts. (Skip this step if using chicken tenders.)

2. Make the marinade by mixing the oil, salt, sugar, garlic, paprika, cumin, coriander, ginger, turmeric, cinnamon, and cayenne in a small bowl or measuring cup. Place the pounded chicken (or tenders) inside a resealable freezer bag (the same one you used for pounding if it's still in good shape). Add the marinade, press the air out of the bag, and seal shut. Massage the marinade into the chicken until evenly coated. Place the bag in a bowl in the refrigerator (the bowl protects against leakage), and marinate the chicken for at least 5 hours or overnight.

3. Make the couscous salad: Bring the chicken broth, butter, and ¼ teaspoon of the salt to a boil in a medium pot. Stir in the couscous. Cover the pot with a tight-fitting lid and remove from the heat. Let sit for 5 minutes, then fluff the couscous immediately with a fork so it doesn't clump together.

4. In a small bowl, whisk together the apricot jam, oil, vinegar, remaining ¼ teaspoon salt, and a few grinds of fresh black pepper. Add about three-fourths of the vinaigrette to the couscous and stir to combine. Taste and add the remaining vinaigrette, little by little if necessary (you may not need all of it). Be sure to add all the little chunks of apricot from the vinaigrette, as they tend to settle at the bottom of the bowl. Stir in the scallions, herbs (if using), and sliced almonds. Taste and adjust the seasoning if necessary. If not serving immediately, refrigerate until ready to serve. Warm up in the microwave or bring to room temperature before serving.

5. Preheat a grill to high heat. Using tongs, dip a wad of paper towels in vegetable oil and carefully wipe the grill grate several times until glossy and coated. Grill the marinated chicken, covered, for 2 to 3 minutes per side, until cooked through (to be sure, make a little cut at the thickest part—it should be opaque in the center). Do not overcook. Serve with the couscous salad.

Barbecued Soy & Ginger Chicken Thighs

WITH SPICY CUCUMBER-PEANUT SALAD

Flavored with soy sauce, ginger, lime, and garam masala (an Indian spice blend), this dish blends ingredients from all over Asia. It's deliciously different, perfect for when you want to fire up the grill and elevate the usual cookout fare. Because of the sugar content in the marinade, the chicken gets gorgeously caramelized and charred on the grill. The salad not only makes a lovely and crunchy side dish, but it's also crazy-good on its own, so go ahead and double the recipe to have extra for lunch the next day (just wait to add the peanuts until right before serving so they don't get soggy). Serve the chicken over steamed rice to soak up the delicious sauce, with the cucumber salad on the side.

Serves 4

FOR THE CHICKEN

6 tablespoons (87 g) packed dark brown sugar

6 tablespoons (90 mL) soy sauce

3 tablespoons fresh lime juice (from 2 limes)

1½ tablespoons vegetable oil, plus more for grilling

½ teaspoon toasted sesame oil

¾ teaspoon garam masala

3 garlic cloves, coarsely chopped

1 (1-inch/2.5 cm) piece fresh ginger, coarsely chopped

½ teaspoon cayenne pepper

8 boneless, skinless chicken thighs (2⅓ pounds/1 kg), trimmed of excess fat and skin (see Pro Tip, page 70)

2 scallions (dark green parts only), thinly sliced, for serving

FOR THE SALAD

2 tablespoons rice wine vinegar

1½ tablespoons smooth peanut butter

1 tablespoon soy sauce

1 tablespoon vegetable oil

1 tablespoon Sambal Oelek or Asian chili-garlic sauce (see Sourcing Savvy, page 116)

1 tablespoon sugar

1 teaspoon toasted sesame oil

½ cup (70 g) very thinly sliced red onion (from 1 small onion; see Pro Tip)

1 English/hothouse cucumber, halved, seeded, and thinly sliced

⅓ cup (47 g) salted peanuts, coarsely chopped

3 tablespoons finely chopped fresh cilantro

-RECIPE CONTINUES-

HEADS UP

Allow at least 3 hours to marinate the chicken.

SOURCING SAVVY

Use good-quality Virginia peanuts if you can find them. Grown primarily in Virginia (but also in North Carolina, South Carolina, and Texas), Virginia peanuts are large, flavorful, and extra crunchy. They are often referred to as "ballpark peanuts" because they are the kind sold at baseball games.

PRO TIPS

As the salad sits, the cucumber will exude water and dilute the dressing. If you have leftovers, you may need to punch up the flavor with a bit more vinegar, soy sauce, and sugar.

Raw onions can be a little overpowering. To tame their bite, place them in a small bowl, cover them with cold water, and let sit for 10 minutes. Drain well and then proceed with your recipe.

1. Marinate the chicken: Combine the brown sugar, soy sauce, lime juice, 1½ tablespoons vegetable oil, the sesame oil, garam masala, garlic, ginger, and cayenne in a blender and puree until completely smooth. Set ¼ cup (60 mL) of the marinade aside, covered; you'll use this later for the sauce. Place the rest of the marinade in a resealable freezer bag along with the chicken thighs. Be sure the chicken is evenly coated with the marinade, press air out of the bag and seal shut, then place the bag in the refrigerator (in a bowl in case of leakage) and marinate for at least 3 hours or overnight.

2. Make the salad: In a medium bowl, combine the vinegar, peanut butter, soy sauce, vegetable oil, Sambal Oelek, sugar, and sesame oil. Whisk until smooth. (The peanut butter will be a little stubborn, but it will eventually break down and combine.) Add the red onion to the dressing and let sit for at least 10 minutes to soften the onion.

3. Grill the chicken: Preheat a grill to high heat. Using tongs, dip a wad of paper towels in vegetable oil and carefully wipe the grill grate several times until glossy and coated to prevent sticking. Place the chicken on the grill, cover, and cook for 5 to 6 minutes per side, until nicely browned and cooked through. Transfer the chicken to a serving platter.

4. Finish the salad: Add the cucumber, peanuts, and cilantro to the bowl with the salad dressing and toss to combine. Taste and adjust the seasoning if necessary.

5. Top the chicken with the reserved marinade and the scallions. Serve with the spicy cucumber salad.

Sheet Pan Roast Chicken

WITH ARTICHOKES, POTATOES, CARROTS & PEAS

Simple prep, easy cleanup: Is there anything more appealing on a weeknight than a sheet-pan supper? This one really delivers. The chicken skin and the potatoes become extra crispy, the artichokes are tangy and caramelized, the peas, carrots, and onions are sweet—and everything is gorgeously flavored with lemony-garlicky olive oil. The recipe comes from my mom's dear friend Joanne Biltekoff, who is like an aunt to me. (If you have made Joanne's wonderful pickle recipe from my first cookbook, you know she can cook!) I considered putting this recipe in the weekend section, since the chicken and vegetables take an hour to roast, but since it only takes 15 minutes to throw together, I decided it qualified as a weeknight supper, so long as you walk in the door at a reasonable hour. That said, I wouldn't hesitate to serve this on a holiday or special occasion.

Serves 4 to 6

1 medium yellow onion, cut into 1-inch (2.5 cm) chunks

4 garlic cloves, coarsely chopped

1 pound (454 g) baby potatoes (see Pro Tip)

2 to 3 carrots, sliced 1½ inches (4 cm) thick on an angle

2 heaping cups (240 g) frozen artichoke hearts (no need to thaw)

1½ tablespoons fresh lemon juice (from 1 lemon)

¼ cup (60 mL) extra-virgin olive oil

2¾ teaspoons salt

½ teaspoon freshly ground black pepper

2 teaspoons dried thyme or herbes de Provence

8 pieces bone-in, skin-on chicken thighs or drumsticks, trimmed of excess skin and fat (about 3 pounds/1.4 kg)

1 teaspoon paprika

1½ cups (180 g) frozen peas (no need to thaw)

¼ cup water

SOURCING SAVVY

Frozen artichokes taste like fresh, steamed artichokes and are far superior to canned or marinated artichokes (both of which have a strong citric acid flavor). They can be a little hard to find; in my area, Trader Joe's and Whole Foods carry them.

PRO TIP

If any of your baby potatoes are especially large, cut them in half.

1. Preheat the oven to 425°F (220°C) and set an oven rack in the middle position.

2. In a large bowl, combine the onion, garlic, potatoes, carrots, artichokes, lemon juice, 3 tablespoons of the oil, ¾ teaspoon of the salt, ¼ teaspoon of the pepper, and 1 teaspoon of the thyme or herbes de Provence; toss well. Transfer the vegetables to a 13 x 18-inch (33 x 46 cm) baking sheet (do not line the pan with foil or parchment).

3. In the same bowl (no need to rinse), combine the chicken and paprika, and add the remaining 1 tablespoon oil, 2 teaspoons salt, ¼ teaspoon pepper, and 1 teaspoon thyme or herbes de Provence. Toss until the chicken is evenly coated.

-RECIPE CONTINUES-

4. Place the chicken, skin side up, on the baking sheet, arranging it around the perimeter of the pan with the vegetables more toward the center (the vegetables may burn around the pan's edges). Bake for 50 minutes. Remove the pan from the oven. Check to make sure the chicken is cooked through (if you make a little cut in the meat, it should appear opaque throughout), then transfer the chicken to a plate and tent with foil.

5. Add the peas and water to the vegetables on the baking sheet. Use a wooden spoon to stir the vegetables, scraping the bottom of the pan to release any browned bits (that's where all the flavor is). Place the vegetables back in the oven and cook until the peas are warmed through, about 5 minutes more. Toss the vegetables with the accumulated juices on the baking sheet. Serve the chicken with the vegetables.

Pecorino & Rosemary–Crusted Chicken

My family loves this crispy chicken dish, so it's easy to recruit sous-chefs to help make it. I usually enlist one of the kids to pound the chicken for me, the other to do the breading, and I sauté the chicken—so we have a little assembly line going. For a light meal, top it with arugula tossed with a little lemon and olive oil, or go the comfort-food route by pairing it with Rustic Parmesan Mashed Potatoes (page 171) and a roasted vegetable (see pages 172–73).

Serves 4

1½ pounds (680 g) boneless, skinless chicken breasts or chicken tenders

Salt and freshly ground black pepper

1¼ cups (75 g) panko bread crumbs

½ cup (50 g) finely grated pecorino Romano cheese

1 tablespoon finely chopped fresh rosemary

½ cup (65 g) all-purpose flour

2 large eggs

Vegetable oil, for cooking

Lemon wedges, for serving

1. Slice the chicken breasts in half horizontally to form flat fillets. Place a fillet in a resealable freezer bag and use a meat mallet or rolling pin to pound to an even ¼-inch (6 mm) thickness. Remove the pounded cutlet and set aside. Repeat with the remaining fillets. (Skip this step if using chicken tenderloins; instead, using the palm of your hand, gently flatten the tenderloins to an even ¼-inch/6 mm thickness.) Season the chicken all over with ¾ teaspoon salt and ½ teaspoon of pepper.

2. In a large shallow bowl, combine the panko, pecorino Romano, rosemary, ½ teaspoon salt, and ¼ teaspoon pepper. Mix well, making sure there are no clumps of cheese. Place the flour in another shallow bowl. Beat the eggs in a third bowl. Set up a breading station in this order: flour, eggs, panko.

3. Dredge the chicken in the flour, coating evenly on both sides; dip it in the beaten egg, letting any excess drip off; then dredge it in the panko mixture, turning and patting to adhere. Place the breaded chicken on a plate.

4. Line a 13 x 18-inch (33 x 46 cm) baking sheet with paper towels. In a large nonstick skillet, heat about ⅛ inch (3 mm) of oil over medium-high heat until shimmering. Place as many pieces of chicken in the skillet as will fit in a single layer and cook until the first side is golden brown, 2 to 3 minutes. Carefully flip the chicken and cook for another 2 to 3 minutes, until golden and cooked through. (Lower the heat if the chicken is browning too quickly.) Place the cooked chicken on the paper towel–lined baking sheet to drain. Cook the remaining chicken in the same manner (you shouldn't need more oil). Transfer the chicken to a serving platter or individual plates. Serve with lemon wedges.

MAKE-AHEAD INSTRUCTIONS

The chicken can be breaded and refrigerated up to 8 hours ahead.

SOURCING SAVVY

I use Japanese panko crumbs for coating the chicken instead of the more traditional Italian-style fine bread crumbs. Panko creates a feathery, crisp crust that stays crispy long after it is cooked, so you don't have to pan-fry the chicken at the very last minute.

PRO TIP

When breading chicken, use one hand for the dry coatings and one hand for the wet. It's much less messy this way.

Chicken Marsala

SOURCING SAVVY

I buy boneless, skinless chicken breasts and pound them thin myself rather than using the ultra-thin sliced cutlets sold at the supermarket, since pounding tenderizes the meat. If you'd like to avoid this step, I suggest using chicken tenders, which are naturally very tender. The presentation won't be quite as traditional, but it saves time.

Marsala is a brandy-fortified wine from Sicily. It will keep in a cool, dry spot for months after opening.

My mother didn't teach me to cook—to this day, she dreads cooking!—but she did teach me to appreciate good food. When I was growing up, we ate out as a family every Friday and Saturday night, at least until my sister and I were teenagers with plans of our own. Our favorite place was That's Amore, a neighborhood Italian restaurant that served enormous family-sized portions for everyone to share. We always ordered the chicken Marsala, which was tender pan-fried chicken cutlets smothered with plump mushrooms and a rich Marsala wine sauce. Though it feels fancy, it's an easy dish to make at home; with just one pan, you can have it on the table in 45 minutes. The recipe makes a lovely sauce that is delicious over pasta, polenta, Rice Pilaf (page 171), or Rustic Parmesan Mashed Potatoes (page 171).

Serves 4

1½ pounds (680 g) boneless, skinless chicken breasts (2 large breasts) or chicken tenders (see Sourcing Savvy)

3 tablespoons all-purpose flour

Salt and freshly ground black pepper

1 tablespoon olive oil

3 tablespoons unsalted butter

1 (8-ounce/227 g) package sliced baby bella (or button) mushrooms

3 tablespoons finely chopped shallot (from 1 medium shallot)

2 garlic cloves, minced

⅔ cup (160 mL) chicken broth

⅔ cup (160 mL) dry Marsala wine

⅔ cup (160 mL) heavy cream

2 teaspoons chopped fresh thyme

2 tablespoons chopped fresh Italian parsley, for serving (optional)

1. Slice the chicken breasts in half horizontally to form 4 flat fillets. Place a fillet in a resealable freezer bag and use a meat mallet or rolling pin to pound it to an even ¼-inch (6 mm) thickness. Remove the pounded cutlet and set aside. Repeat with the remaining 3 fillets. (Skip this step if using chicken tenderloins; instead, using the palm of your hand, gently flatten the tenderloins to an even ¼-inch/6 mm thickness.)

2. Place the flour, ¾ teaspoon salt, and ¼ teaspoon pepper in a resealable freezer bag (use the same one you used for pounding if it's still in good shape). Add the chicken to the bag, seal it tightly, and shake to coat the chicken evenly. Set aside.

3. Heat the oil and 2 tablespoons of the butter in a large skillet over medium-high heat. Shake off any excess flour from the chicken fillets and place them in the pan. Cook, turning once, until the chicken is golden on both sides and just barely cooked through, 5 to 6 minutes total. Transfer the chicken to a plate and set aside.

4. Melt the remaining tablespoon butter in the pan. Add the mushrooms and cook, stirring frequently, until they begin to brown, 3 to 4 minutes. Add the shallot, garlic, and ¼ teaspoon of salt; cook until the garlic is fragrant, 1 to 2 minutes more. Add the broth, Marsala, cream, thyme, ¼ teaspoon salt, and ⅛ teaspoon of pepper; use a wooden spoon to scrape any browned bits from the pan into the liquid. Bring to a boil, then reduce the heat to medium and simmer, uncovered, until the sauce is reduced by about half, slightly thickened, and darkened in color, 10 to 15 minutes. (You're going for a thin cream sauce; it won't start to thicken until the very end of the cooking time.) Add the chicken back to the pan, along with any juices that accumulated on the plate. Reduce the heat to low and simmer until the chicken is warmed through and the sauce thickens a bit more, 2 to 3 minutes. Sprinkle with parsley, if using, and serve.

Creamy Dijon Chicken
WITH PEAS

Made with a splash of white wine, heavy cream, and a generous spoonful of Dijon mustard, this dish is *très français*. It is one of the first dishes I learned to make in culinary school because it illustrates two basic French cooking techniques: how to sauté and how to make a white wine cream sauce. I usually make this on Friday night, since it gives me an excuse to open a bottle of wine for the weekend—a splash for the sauce, the rest for us! Serve over Rice Pilaf (page 171) or buttered egg noodles.

Serves 4

1½ pounds (680 g) chicken tenders, tendons trimmed, cut into 1½-inch (4 cm) pieces

1 teaspoon salt

¼ teaspoon freshly ground black pepper

3 tablespoons all-purpose flour

2 tablespoons unsalted butter

1 tablespoon vegetable oil

½ cup (60 g) chopped shallot (from 1 large shallot)

2 garlic cloves, minced

½ cup (120 mL) dry white wine

1 cup (240 mL) heavy cream

½ cup (120 mL) chicken broth

1½ tablespoons Dijon mustard

⅔ cup (80 g) frozen peas

1 teaspoon chopped fresh thyme, or ¼ teaspoon dried

1. Pat the chicken dry with a paper towel. In a medium bowl or pie plate, toss the chicken pieces with ¾ teaspoon of the salt, the pepper, and the flour.

2. In a large (12-inch/30 cm) nonstick skillet, melt the butter over medium-high heat and then add the vegetable oil. When the fat is very hot, add the chicken in a single layer and cook, without stirring, until lightly golden, about 3 minutes. Using tongs, turn the chicken over and cook until just cooked through, 2 to 3 minutes more. Using a slotted spoon, transfer the chicken to a plate and set aside while you make the sauce.

3. Add the shallot to the fat in the pan and reduce the heat to low. Cook, stirring frequently, until the shallot is translucent, about 2 minutes. Add the garlic and cook, stirring constantly, for 1 minute more. Do not brown. Add the wine, increase the heat to high, and boil until mostly evaporated, 3 to 4 minutes. Add the cream, broth, mustard, and the remaining ¼ teaspoon salt; reduce the heat to medium and gently boil until the sauce is slightly reduced and thick enough to lightly coat the back of a spoon, 3 to 5 minutes. Add the peas and the chicken (along with any accumulated juices) and simmer until just warmed through, a few minutes. Stir in the thyme, then taste and adjust the seasoning if necessary. (If the sauce seems too thick, thin it with a bit of water.)

SOURCING SAVVY

When a recipe calls for wine, select a bottle that is inexpensive but still good enough to drink. If you don't want to open a large bottle, look for mini bottles that are sold in four-packs and contain about ¾ cup (160 mL) of wine per bottle; they are ideal for cooking. Always avoid "cooking wines," as they contain salt and other additives.

PRO TIP

To avoid wasting broth when you need only a small amount for a recipe, you can freeze the rest in an airtight container for future use. For a great space-saving option, pour the broth into a resealable freezer bag and lay it flat in the freezer. You can also freeze smaller portions in an ice cube tray. Another option is to use bouillon, a dehydrated broth that comes in the form of granules or paste.

Butter-Style Chicken

WITH MANGO CHUTNEY

SOURCING SAVVY

Garam masala is a traditional and warming Indian spice blend made from ground coriander, black pepper, cumin, cardamom, and cinnamon. Indian markets and most large supermarkets carry it. For a completely different flavor that is equally as delicious, you can try this dish with curry powder instead of garam masala.

PRO TIP

This dish is traditionally cooked with ghee, a type of clarified Indian butter that has a higher smoke point than plain butter. Since I don't have ghee on hand in my kitchen and butter burns over high heat, I use a combination of butter and oil to sauté the chicken. (The oil raises the smoke point of the fat by preventing the milk solids in the butter from burning.)

Butter chicken is a staple menu item in many Indian restaurants in the U.S. According to legend, it was created when a restaurateur in India combined leftover chicken with a tomato sauce enriched with butter and cream. Traditionally, the chicken for this dish is marinated in yogurt, lemon, and spices and then cooked in a clay oven called a tandoor. To save time, I sauté unmarinated chicken in a skillet and then briefly simmer it in a rich, spice-infused sauce. This results in ultra-tender chicken. In fact, one of my recipe testers remarked that this must be called "butter chicken" because the chicken is so tender it's like "buttah!"

Along with basmati rice or naan, I love a little mango chutney on the side; it adds a delicious gingery sweetness that complements the chicken.

Serves 4

1½ pounds (680 g) chicken tenders, tendons trimmed, cut into 1½-inch (4 cm) pieces

1¼ teaspoons salt

2 teaspoons garam masala

3 tablespoons all-purpose flour

2 tablespoons unsalted butter

1 tablespoon vegetable oil

1 medium yellow onion, finely chopped (about 1 cup/140 g)

1½ tablespoons finely chopped fresh ginger (from a 2-inch/5 cm knob)

1 teaspoon ground coriander

1¾ teaspoons ground cumin

⅛ teaspoon cayenne pepper (optional)

1 (8-ounce/227 g) can tomato sauce

1 cup (240 mL) heavy cream

¾ teaspoon sugar

¼ teaspoon freshly ground black pepper

3 tablespoons water

3 tablespoons chopped fresh cilantro (optional)

Basmati rice, for serving

Mango chutney, such as Major Grey's, for serving

1. Pat the chicken dry with a paper towel. In a medium bowl, sprinkle the chicken pieces evenly with ¾ teaspoon of the salt and 1 teaspoon of the garam masala; toss to coat evenly. Add the flour and toss again, making sure the chicken is well coated.

2. In a large (12-inch/30 cm) nonstick skillet, heat 1 tablespoon of the butter and the oil over medium-high heat. When the fat is hot and shimmering, add the chicken in a single layer and cook, without stirring, until it is lightly golden on the underside, about 3 minutes. Using tongs, turn the chicken pieces over and cook until just cooked through, 2 to 3 minutes more. Transfer the chicken to a plate and set it aside while you make the sauce (you'll use the skillet in the next step—there's no need to wash it).

3. Melt the remaining tablespoon butter in the same skillet over medium heat. Add the onion and ginger and cook, stirring frequently, until softened, 3 to 4 minutes. If the onion starts to brown, reduce the heat. Add the coriander, cumin, cayenne (if using), and the remaining teaspoon garam masala; stir and cook 1 minute more. Add the tomato sauce, cream, sugar, pepper, water, and the remaining ½ teaspoon salt. Bring to a gentle boil, then reduce the heat and simmer, uncovered, until slightly thickened, about 3 minutes.

4. Add the chicken, along with any accumulated juices, to the sauce and simmer just a few minutes until the chicken is warmed through. Taste the sauce and adjust the seasoning if necessary. Sprinkle with the cilantro, if using, and serve with basmati rice and mango chutney. (Note that the sauce will thicken as it sits; thin it with a bit of water if necessary.)

From the Sea

Everyday Spice–Crusted Salmon WITH TARTAR SAUCE

MAKE-AHEAD INSTRUCTIONS

The tartar sauce can be made a day ahead and refrigerated.

PRO TIPS

You can roast some broccoli directly on the baking sheet with the salmon. Simply toss about 5 cups (375 g) of 1½-inch (4 cm) broccoli florets (from a 1-pound/454 g head) with 2 tablespoons olive oil and a heaping ¼ teaspoon salt. Arrange the florets around the salmon and proceed with the recipe.

The salmon skin will stick to the foil; this is intentional, as it makes it easy to separate the meat from the skin. If you'd like to be able to transfer the whole fillet to a serving platter, use parchment paper instead of aluminum foil.

Ever since I discovered the spice blend used for this recipe (which, by the way, is a copycat of Trader Joe's Everyday Seasoning, hence the title), I keep a jarful in my pantry. Sprinkled over a side of salmon, it makes a fabulously easy weeknight dinner that also feels a little special. I know it seems like extra work to grind whole spices rather than buying them already ground, but the coarse texture of freshly ground spices creates a lovely crust that really enhances the dish. Note that the recipe makes about ⅓ cup of the spice blend and is enough to make this dish twice. Store the extra in a sealable plastic bag or glass jar in the pantry. (And if you're wondering what to do with any leftover mustard and coriander seeds, check out the refrigerator pickle recipe on my website.) A big thank-you to my lovely reader, Sherri Ferrell, who shared this recipe with me. The salmon is really good with roasted broccoli, which you can roast right on the baking sheet with the fish (see Pro Tip), and Rice Pilaf (page 171).

Serves 4 to 6

FOR THE SALMON

1 tablespoon black peppercorns

1 tablespoon mustard seeds

2 teaspoons dried minced onion

2 teaspoons dried minced garlic

1¾ teaspoons kosher salt

1 teaspoon coriander seeds

1 teaspoon red pepper flakes

1 (2½-pound/1.1 kg) skin-on salmon fillet, pin bones removed

2 tablespoons extra-virgin olive oil

Lemon wedges, for serving

FOR THE TARTAR SAUCE

1 cup (240 g) best-quality mayonnaise, such as Hellmann's or Duke's

2 tablespoons capers, drained and chopped

1½ tablespoons minced shallot (from 1 small shallot)

2 teaspoons fresh lemon juice (from 1 lemon)

2 tablespoons sweet pickle relish

¾ teaspoon Worcestershire sauce

½ teaspoon Dijon mustard

¼ teaspoon freshly ground black pepper

1. Preheat the oven to 450°F (235°C) and set an oven rack in the middle position. Line a baking sheet with heavy-duty aluminum foil (see Pro Tip).

2. Make the salmon: In a spice grinder (or a blender), combine the peppercorns, mustard seeds, dried onion, dried garlic, salt, coriander seeds, and red pepper flakes. Process for a few seconds until coarsely ground.

-RECIPE CONTINUES-

3. Place the salmon, skin side down, on the prepared baking sheet and coat it with the oil. Sprinkle it evenly with 2½ tablespoons of the spice mixture (reserve the rest of the spice mixture for another time). Roast until the salmon is cooked to your liking, 14 to 16 minutes for medium (if your fillet is extra thin, start checking it after 10 minutes; use a paring knife to flake a thicker part of the fillet).

4. Make the tartar sauce: Meanwhile, in a medium bowl, whisk together the mayonnaise, capers, shallot, lemon juice, relish, Worcestershire sauce, mustard, and pepper. Taste and adjust seasoning if necessary.

5. Use a thin, wide spatula to cut the salmon into serving pieces—the flesh should easily lift from the skin. Serve with the tartar sauce and lemon wedges.

Red Snapper & Snow Peas in Coconut Curry Broth

Served over fragrant jasmine rice, this is a flavorful and light, not to mention stunning, supper inspired by the classic Thai green curry dishes that bring your main dish and veggies together in one bowl. The fish and snow peas are gently poached in a rich and gingery coconut curry broth, which infuses them with lovely flavor. I love red snapper for this dish, but it can be pricey; if you'd prefer a less expensive option, tilapia or Atlantic cod will work nicely. And, if possible, have the fishmonger remove the skin while you're at the store. If you need to do it yourself, see the Sourcing Savvy on page 146 for instructions. • PHOTOGRAPH ON PAGE 138

Serves 4

1½ pounds (680 g) red snapper fillets, skin removed, cut into 1½-inch (4 cm) chunks

½ teaspoon salt

2 tablespoons vegetable oil

1 bunch of scallions (light and dark green parts separated), thinly sliced

1½ tablespoons finely chopped fresh ginger (from a 1½-inch/4 cm knob)

1 red bell pepper, seeded and thinly sliced into bite-sized pieces

2½ tablespoons Thai green curry paste

1 (13.5-ounce/400 mL) can full-fat coconut milk (do not use low-fat)

2 tablespoons fish sauce

2 tablespoons (packed) light brown sugar

1 tablespoon fresh lime juice (from 1 lime)

4 ounces (113 g) snow peas, trimmed (see Pro Tip)

¼ cup (10 g) thinly sliced fresh Thai or Italian basil

Cooked jasmine rice, for serving

1. Sprinkle the fish evenly with the salt; set aside.

2. Heat the oil in a large skillet over medium heat. Add the light scallions, the ginger, and bell pepper and cook, stirring constantly, until softened and fragrant, about 4 minutes. Add the curry paste and cook, stirring constantly, for 1 minute more. Add the coconut milk, fish sauce, brown sugar, and lime juice; bring to a boil. Add the snow peas and red snapper; spoon the sauce over the fish.

3. Bring the broth to a gentle boil, then reduce the heat to low and simmer, covered, turning the fish once halfway through, until the fish is cooked through, about 5 minutes. Sprinkle with the basil and the dark scallions. Taste and adjust the seasoning if necessary. Serve with jasmine rice.

SOURCING SAVVY

Curry paste can be spicy and varies by brand. I use Thai Kitchen, which is mild. If using a different brand, add it little by little to taste.

PRO TIPS

You may find that when you open a can of coconut milk, a solid white cream covers the top. Since this recipe calls for a whole can, you don't need to worry about stirring it before using; simply add the separated coconut milk to the pan and stir it to re-emulsify.

———

Snow peas have tough, string-like fibers running along their seams (the straight edge) that should be removed. Use your fingertips to snap off the stem end of the snow pea, leaving the stringy part attached. Use the partially disconnected end to pull off and remove the string. If the string breaks before you've removed it all, repeat the process using the other end of the pea. (Or look for snow peas already trimmed in the produce department; they're a great timesaver.)

Greek-Style Shrimp

WITH TOMATOES & FETA

Inspired by shrimp saganaki, the classic Greek dish of shrimp in a spicy tomato sauce with feta cheese, this dish is made almost entirely from pantry and freezer staples. It's one of my go-to meals when I have to hit the kitchen running. You begin by making a quick tomato sauce on the stovetop. Then, you nestle the shrimp in the sauce, top it with chunks of feta, and slide it into the oven to bake. Before serving, you flash the pan under the broiler to brown the feta and then sprinkle fresh mint over the top to finish it off. The sauce is plentiful and packed with flavor, so be sure to serve lots of crusty bread on the side to sop it up.

Serves 4

¼ cup (60 mL) extra-virgin olive oil

¾ cup (90 g) finely chopped shallot (from 2 large shallots)

4 garlic cloves, roughly chopped

1 (28-ounce/794 g) can diced tomatoes, with their juice

1½ teaspoons salt

¼ teaspoon freshly ground black pepper

1 teaspoon ground cumin

½ teaspoon red pepper flakes (use less if you are heat-sensitive)

1 tablespoon honey

1½ pounds (680 g) extra-large (26/30) shrimp, peeled and deveined

6 ounces (170 g) feta cheese

¾ teaspoon dried oregano

2 tablespoons roughly chopped fresh mint

PRO TIP

If you do not have an ovenproof skillet or if you'd like to serve this in a pretty dish, simply transfer the tomato sauce to a 9 x 13-inch (23 x 33 cm) or equivalent (3-quart/3 L) broiler-safe baking dish and proceed from there.

1. Preheat the oven to 400°F (205°C); set one oven rack in the middle position and another about 5 inches underneath the broiler.

2. Heat the oil in a wide ovenproof skillet (see Pro Tip) over medium-low heat. Add the shallots and garlic and cook, stirring occasionally, until softened, 5 to 7 minutes. Do not brown. Add the tomatoes with their juices, salt, pepper, cumin, red pepper flakes, and honey. Bring to a boil, then reduce the heat to medium low and cook, uncovered, stirring occasionally, until the sauce is thickened, 15 to 20 minutes.

3. Off the heat, arrange the shrimp over the tomato sauce in an even layer. Crumble the feta over the shrimp, and then sprinkle with the oregano. Bake on the middle rack of the oven for 12 to 15 minutes, until the shrimp are pink and just cooked (the cooking time will depend on the size of the shrimp).

4. Turn on the broiler. Using an oven mitt, carefully transfer the pan to the higher oven rack and broil for 1 to 2 minutes, or until the feta is golden brown in spots. Using an oven mitt, remove the pan from the oven (and immediately place the oven mitt over the handle of the pan, because it's easy to forget that it is burning hot). Let the shrimp rest for 5 minutes, then sprinkle with the mint and serve.

Pan-Seared Halibut

WITH BEURRE BLANC

SOURCING SAVVY

Tarragon, with its sweet, anise-like flavor, is an essential herb in French cooking. Many supermarkets carry it, but if you can't find it, fresh thyme is a good alternative.

Ask your fishmonger to remove the skin from the halibut and cut the fish into portions. If you need to remove the skin yourself, hold a very sharp chef's knife so that the blade is parallel to the cutting board and make a small incision between the skin and the flesh on one end of the fillet. Hold on to the flap of the skin and pull in one direction while gently cutting between the flesh and the skin moving in the other direction. Check your work as you're going to ensure you don't cut away too much of the flesh. (It's important to cut the fish into serving portions before cooking; otherwise, it won't cook evenly.)

PRO TIP

Resist the urge to fiddle with the fillets as they cook. Letting the fish sear untouched in the hot oil creates that lovely, flavorful golden crust that makes this dish restaurant-worthy.

When cooking a beautiful fish like halibut, it's best to keep the preparation simple to let the fish really shine. One of my favorite ways to make it is to pan-sear the fillets until golden, then top them with a classic French beurre blanc or white wine butter sauce. I know the sauce sounds fancy, but it's foolproof, easy to whip up in 10 minutes, and makes the fish taste like something you'd pay *beaucoup* bucks for at a high-end restaurant.

The beurre blanc will hold for about 30 minutes, so feel free to get a little head start. I usually serve this dish with a steamed vegetable and Rice Pilaf (page 171).

Serves 4

FOR THE BEURRE BLANC

1 cup (240 mL) dry white wine

⅓ cup (40 g) minced shallot (from 1 large shallot)

¼ cup (60 mL) heavy cream

½ cup (1 stick/4 ounces/113 g) cold unsalted butter, cut into 8 pieces

1 tablespoon fresh lemon juice (from 1 lemon)

1 tablespoon chopped fresh chives

1 teaspoon chopped fresh tarragon

¼ teaspoon salt

⅛ teaspoon freshly ground black pepper

FOR THE FISH

4 (6-ounce/170 g) skinless halibut fillets (see Sourcing Savvy)

¾ teaspoon salt

½ teaspoon freshly ground black pepper

1 tablespoon extra-virgin olive oil

1 tablespoon unsalted butter

1. Make the beurre blanc: In a 2- to 3-quart (2 to 3 L) saucepan, combine the wine and shallot. Boil over high heat until the wine is reduced to about 2 tablespoons, 6 to 8 minutes. Add the cream and boil for 1 minute. Reduce the heat to low, and then gradually add the butter, one piece at a time, whisking constantly, until melted (wait until each piece is melted before adding the next). When all the butter is incorporated, stir in the lemon juice, chives, tarragon, salt, and pepper. Taste and adjust the seasoning if necessary. (Keep in mind the sauce will have a creamy consistency, but it will not be thick.) Cover to keep warm and set aside.

2. Cook the fish: Season the halibut all over with the salt and pepper. Heat the oil and butter in a large nonstick skillet over medium-high heat until hot and shimmering. Place the fish, presentation side down, in the pan and cook, undisturbed, until golden brown and crisp, 3 to 4 minutes. Flip the fish and reduce the heat to medium; continue cooking until the halibut is just firm to the touch and opaque when you pry open a thicker piece with a paring knife, 3 to 4 minutes. Transfer the cooked halibut to a serving platter or plates, spoon the beurre blanc over top, and serve.

Miso & Soy Marinated Black Cod

This is my "weeknight" take on the ubiquitous miso-marinated black cod made popular by the chef Nobu Matsuhisa. While the original recipe requires several days of marinating time, this one calls for only 30 minutes. The main difference is that instead of using sake in the marinade, I use soy sauce and sesame oil to infuse flavor quickly. The sweet, salty, umami-rich marinade does double duty: half of it is used to marinate the fish and the other half serves as a drizzling sauce.

Serves 4

½ cup (120 mL) mirin

¼ cup plus 2 tablespoons (98 g) white miso paste

¼ cup (50 g) sugar

2 teaspoons toasted sesame oil

3 to 5 tablespoons (90 mL) soy sauce

4 (6- to 8-ounce/170 to 227 g) 1-inch-thick (2.5 cm) skinless Pacific black cod loins or Chilean sea bass fillets

1. Make the marinade: In a blender or mini food processor, blend the mirin, miso paste, sugar, sesame oil, and 3 tablespoons of the soy sauce. Taste and, if necessary, add the remaining soy sauce, little by little, until you have a pleasant balance of salty and sweet. Pour half the marinade into a small microwave-safe bowl (this will be your sauce). Pour the remaining marinade into a baking dish large enough to hold the fish in a single layer. Add the fish to the marinade, turning to coat evenly, and let it sit at room temperature for 30 to 35 minutes (no longer than that or the fish will get too salty).

2. Set one oven rack 6 inches beneath the broiler and another rack in the center of the oven. Preheat the broiler. Line a 13 x 18-inch (33 x 46 cm) baking sheet with heavy-duty aluminum foil.

3. Place the marinated fish, presentation side up, on the prepared baking sheet (do not pour the marinade over the fish; it will burn and smoke in the oven). Broil for 3 to 5 minutes, until the top is bubbling and caramel colored. Turn off the broiler and set the oven temperature to 350°F (175°C). (The oven should come to temperature immediately, as the broiler has been on.) Move the baking sheet to the center rack and finish cooking for 3 to 6 minutes more, until the fish is opaque and flakes easily with a fork.

4. Meanwhile, warm the reserved marinade in the microwave for about 30 seconds. Transfer the fish to a serving platter or plates and drizzle with a bit of the sauce (be judicious; a little goes a long way). Pass the remaining sauce at the table.

SOURCING SAVVY

Miso paste, a common ingredient in Japanese cuisine, is made from fermented soybeans. It has a rich umami flavor and a consistency similar to peanut butter. There are a few different varieties of miso paste—white, yellow, and red. White miso is fairly sweet and mellow, yellow a bit earthier, and red tends to be the most robust and salty.

Pacific black cod, also known as sablefish or butterfish, is a mild and buttery white fish with a silky texture and large flakes. I like to use the loin, which is the prime cut from the middle and fattest part of the fillet, as it is usually sold boneless and skinless (the whole fillets have many pin bones that are difficult to remove before cooking). If you can't find the loin, Chilean sea bass makes an excellent substitute. Serve with steamed rice.

Hawaiian-Style Tuna Poke Bowls

Many years ago, after visiting our son at sleepaway camp during the summer, Michael and I spent a weekend at a spa resort in the Poconos. We both loved the resort's take on tuna poke (pronounced po-kay), a traditional Hawaiian salad of marinated raw tuna with sushi rice and lots of toppings, so I came up with this similar version when we got home. The resort dish was served with crispy-fried wontons; to keep things weeknight streamlined, I put potato chips on mine instead! They make a delicious (and easy) addition.

Serves 4 to 6

6 tablespoons (90 mL) soy sauce

2 tablespoons vegetable oil

1 tablespoon toasted sesame oil

2 tablespoons honey

1 tablespoon Sambal Oelek or Asian chili-garlic sauce (see Sourcing Savvy, page 116)

2 teaspoons grated fresh ginger (from a 1-inch/2.5 cm knob)

3 scallions (light and dark green parts), thinly sliced

1 pound (454 g) sushi-grade ahi tuna (yellowfin or big-eye tuna), diced into ¼-inch (6 mm) pieces

2 cups (400 g) sushi rice, cooked according to package instructions (or any other type of rice or grain)

OPTIONAL TOPPINGS

Sliced avocado

Sliced cucumber

Edamame

Pickled ginger

Diced mango

Potato chips or wonton crisps

Sesame seeds

1. In a medium bowl, whisk together the soy sauce, vegetable oil, sesame oil, honey, Sambal Oelek, ginger, and scallions. Add the tuna and gently toss. Let the mixture sit in the refrigerator for at least 15 minutes or up to 1 hour (no longer or it will get too salty).

2. To serve, scoop the rice into bowls, top with the tuna, then add your desired toppings. Serve the sauce/marinade on the side, for drizzling over the toppings.

Baked Salmon

WITH HONEY MUSTARD & PECAN-PANKO CRUST

This elegant baked salmon dish takes a total of 20 minutes: 10 minutes to prepare and 10 minutes to bake. It's perfect for when you have company coming at the end of a long day (and are asking yourself, "What was I thinking?") or on a busy weeknight when you're pressed for time. To parents of picky eaters: if your kids are lukewarm on fish, I find that a crunchy coating is the best way to entice them (you can omit the nuts and double the panko, if need be). If you'd like to get a head start, the salmon can be glazed, coated with the panko-pecan mixture, and refrigerated up to 3 hours ahead of time.

Serves 4

Nonstick cooking spray

2 tablespoons Dijon mustard

2 tablespoons unsalted butter, melted

1 tablespoon honey

¾ teaspoon salt

¼ teaspoon freshly ground black pepper

¼ cup (15 g) panko bread crumbs

¼ cup (30 g) finely chopped pecans

2 teaspoons finely chopped fresh Italian parsley (optional, for color)

4 (6-ounce/170 g) salmon fillets

1 lemon, for serving (optional)

1. Preheat the oven to 450°F (235°C) and set an oven rack in the middle position. Line a baking sheet with aluminum foil for easy cleanup, and spray the foil with nonstick cooking spray.

2. In a small bowl, whisk together the mustard, melted butter, honey, ½ teaspoon of the salt, and the pepper.

3. In another small bowl, mix the panko, pecans, parsley (if using), and the remaining ¼ teaspoon salt.

4. Spoon the honey-mustard mixture evenly over the salmon fillets. (Don't worry if it drips down the sides a little.) Sprinkle the panko-pecan mixture over the glaze, pressing it lightly so it adheres.

5. Bake for 7 to 10 minutes per inch of thickness, depending on how well done you like your salmon. (If you find that the topping is browning too fast, loosely cover the salmon with foil.) Serve hot or at room temperature. (Note that if your salmon has skin, it may stick to the foil; to remove the fish from the pan, slide a thin spatula between the skin and the flesh, leaving the skin behind.)

Meaty Mains

Bulgogi-Style Flank Steak Skewers

HEADS UP

Allow at least 1 hour to marinate the steak.

PRO TIPS

If you only have wooden skewers, you'll need to soak them in water for at least 20 minutes prior to threading the food on to keep them from burning once they hit the grill (or you can cover the tips of the skewers with small pieces of foil). If you grill frequently and want to skip that extra step, metal skewers are a small but worthwhile investment; they don't require soaking and are endlessly reusable.

Freezing the beef for about 30 minutes before slicing will make it firmer and easier to slice.

Is there anything better than hearing "Mom, this is SO good" at the dinner table? That's what happens whenever I serve these bulgogi-inspired soy sauce and brown sugar–marinated steak skewers. They get devoured with gusto, and there are never any leftovers. Bulgogi is a Korean barbecue dish of thin, marinated slices of meat cooked on a grill or stove-top griddle. The marinade both infuses the steak with salty, sweet, spicy flavor and also helps the steak caramelize nicely on the grill. Be sure to get the grill very hot and cook only 2 minutes per side. You want nice char in the short time it takes to cook these; flank steak gets tough when it is cooked beyond medium-rare.

Serves 4

2 pounds (907 g) flank steak, sliced about ¼ inch (6 mm) thick across the grain (see Pro Tip)

¼ cup (60 mL) vegetable oil, plus more for grilling

½ cup (120 mL) soy sauce

6 tablespoons (87 g) packed dark brown sugar

4 large garlic cloves, roughly chopped

¼ cup (30 g) roughly chopped shallot (from 1 medium shallot)

¾ teaspoon red pepper flakes

2 scallions (dark green parts only), thinly sliced, for serving (optional)

Rice, for serving

1. Thread the sliced steak onto long skewers in an accordion fashion, leaving a little space between the folds to ensure even heat circulation. Lay the skewers flat in a large baking dish.

2. Combine the ¼ cup (60 mL) oil, the soy sauce, brown sugar, garlic, shallot, and red pepper flakes in a blender and puree until smooth and thickened. Pour half the mixture (about ½ cup/120 mL) over the meat skewers and turn to coat evenly. Cover with plastic wrap and marinate in the refrigerator for at least 1 hour or overnight, flipping the skewers halfway through. Transfer the remaining marinade to a container; cover and refrigerate until later (this will be your sauce).

3. Preheat a grill to high heat.

4. In a small saucepan, bring the reserved marinade to a gentle boil; reduce the heat to low and simmer, covered, for 5 minutes.

5. Using tongs, dip a wad of paper towels in vegetable oil and carefully wipe the grill grate several times, until glossy and coated, to prevent sticking. Grill the skewers, covered, until the beef is browned on the outside but still pink on the inside, about 2 minutes per side. Transfer the skewers to a serving platter and drizzle with the warm marinade. Sprinkle with scallions, if using, and serve with rice.

Flat Iron Carne Asada

BLOG FAVE

The carne asada, or Mexican-style grilled steak, at my favorite Mexican restaurant is made with skirt steak, but when I make carne asada at home, I prefer to use flat iron steak. It's an affordable, widely available cut that's almost as tender as filet mignon, and it's ideal for high-heat, quick-cooking methods like grilling. The main ingredient in my marinade is soy sauce, which may seem unusual, but it enhances the umami (meaty/savory) flavor of the meat. Additionally, the sugar in the marinade encourages caramelization on the grill, which amps up the flavor even more. You'll likely need to buy two flat iron steaks, but even if you're able to find a large one, it's best to cut it in half; the steaks will cook faster and you'll have more surface area to char on the grill. My family fights over the charred end pieces!

Serves 4 to 6

¼ cup (60 mL) soy sauce

3 tablespoons fresh lime juice (from 2 limes)

3 tablespoons vegetable oil, plus more for grilling

1 tablespoon sugar

1 teaspoon ground cumin

1½ teaspoons ancho chile powder

3 large garlic cloves, finely minced

2 pounds (907 g) flat iron steak

HEADS UP

Allow at least 4 hours to marinate the steak.

1. In a dish large enough to hold the steak, whisk together the soy sauce, lime juice, 3 tablespoons oil, the sugar, cumin, chile powder, and garlic.

2. Using a fork, poke holes about 1 inch (2.5 cm) apart all over the steak on one side only. Place the steak in the marinade and turn to coat evenly (it doesn't matter which side is up). Cover and refrigerate for at least 4 hours or overnight, turning the steak at least once.

3. Preheat a grill to high heat. Using tongs, dip a wad of paper towels in vegetable oil and carefully wipe the grill grate several times until glossy and coated. Grill the steak, covered, for 5 to 6 minutes per side for medium-rare. Let the meat rest on a cutting board, tented with aluminum foil, for about 5 minutes. Thinly slice the steak against the grain and serve.

Grilled Italian Sausages
WITH SWEET & TANGY PEPPERS

PRO TIP

The key to juicy, perfectly cooked grilled sausage is to cook the links over direct heat to brown the exterior and then to move them to indirect heat to finish the cooking. This prevents the exterior from burning before the inside is cooked through, and it also prevents the juices inside the sausage (the fat, really) from boiling while cooking, which can cause the sausages to split and the juices to run out. (Never prick the sausages!)

Grilled sausage is almost impossible to mess up—it comes perfectly seasoned and its fat content ensures juiciness, even if slightly overcooked—so this is a guaranteed delicious, stress-free dish for a weeknight dinner or a casual cookout. What's more, assuming you have a few staples in your pantry, the meal couldn't be easier to shop for: 3 bell peppers, an onion, a few packs of sausage, and you're done! The sausage and peppers can be served as is or tucked into a hoagie roll.

Serves 4 to 6

2 tablespoons extra-virgin olive oil

1 large red onion, halved and cut into ¼-inch (6 mm) slices

3 large bell peppers (preferably a combination of colors), stemmed, seeded, and cut into ¼-inch (6 mm) strips

¾ teaspoon salt

½ teaspoon freshly ground black pepper

1 (14.5-ounce/411 g) can diced tomatoes, with their juice

1 teaspoon sugar

2 teaspoons balsamic vinegar

¼ cup (10 g) chopped fresh basil (optional)

Vegetable oil, for grilling

2 pounds (907 g) hot Italian sausage links

1. Heat the oil in a large skillet over medium-high heat. Add the onion, peppers, salt, and pepper. Cook, uncovered, stirring frequently, until the onion and peppers are slightly browned, 10 to 12 minutes. Add the tomatoes and sugar and reduce the heat to medium; continue cooking, stirring occasionally, until the peppers are soft, 8 to 10 minutes more. Stir in the vinegar and basil (if using), then taste and adjust the seasoning if necessary.

2. Meanwhile, preheat a grill to medium heat. Using tongs, dip a wad of paper towels in vegetable oil and carefully wipe the grill grate several times until glossy and coated. Grill the sausages over direct heat, covered, turning occasionally and moving to indirect heat once browned all over, until cooked through, 8 to 12 minutes. Serve the sausages with the peppers on the side.

HOW TO COOK SAUSAGES INDOORS

If you don't have grilling weather, you can cook the sausages on the stovetop. Heat 1 tablespoon of vegetable oil in a large nonstick skillet over medium-high heat. Add the sausages and cook, turning frequently, until evenly browned, about 5 minutes. Reduce the heat to medium low and carefully add ½ cup (120 mL) of water to the skillet. Cover and simmer for about 12 minutes, or until the sausages are cooked through.

Hoisin Pork & Vegetable Rice Bowls

Inspired by the flavors of moo shu pork, the popular Chinese restaurant dish of stir-fried pork, mushrooms, and cabbage, this is a quick, affordable, packed-with-veggies meal that also makes great leftovers. The dish is a bit spicy; feel free to reduce the Sambal Oelek (not a traditional Chinese ingredient, but a great Indonesian pantry staple for when you want to add spicy flavor), if necessary. For variation, instead of serving over rice, try stuffing the pork and vegetable mixture into lettuce cups or flour tortillas.

Serves 4

½ cup (120 mL) chicken broth

½ cup (160 g) best-quality hoisin sauce (such as Lee Kum Kee), plus more for serving

2 tablespoons soy sauce

2 tablespoons Sambal Oelek or Asian chili-garlic sauce, plus more for serving (see Sourcing Savvy, page 116)

2 teaspoons cornstarch

2 tablespoons vegetable oil

1 pound (454 g) ground pork

4 ounces (113 g) shiitake mushrooms, thinly sliced (2 cups)

1 bunch of scallions (light and dark green parts separated), thinly sliced

4 garlic cloves, finely chopped

1½ tablespoons finely chopped fresh ginger (from a 1½-inch/4 cm knob)

1 (10-ounce/283 g) bag shredded cabbage blend, preferably with carrots (4 cups)

Rice, for serving

1. In a medium bowl, whisk together the chicken broth, hoisin sauce, soy sauce, Sambal Oelek, and cornstarch until smooth.

2. Heat 1 tablespoon of the oil in a large nonstick skillet over medium-high heat. Add the pork and cook, stirring constantly and breaking it apart, until just cooked through, 3 to 5 minutes. Use a slotted spoon to transfer the pork to a plate, leaving the fat in the pan.

3. Add the mushrooms to the pan and cook until lightly browned, a few minutes. Add the remaining tablespoon oil and then the light green scallions, the garlic, and ginger. Cook, stirring frequently, for about 2 minutes. Add the shredded cabbage blend and cook until just beginning to wilt, about 1 minute.

4. Add the pork and the sauce to the pan and cook, stirring to combine, until the sauce thickens, about 1 minute. Taste and adjust the seasoning if necessary. Sprinkle the dark green scallions over top. Serve over rice and pass hoisin sauce and Sambal Oelek at the table.

Pan-Seared Filet Mignon
WITH RED WINE SAUCE

SOURCING SAVVY

When a recipe calls for dry red wine, Merlot, Pinot Noir, Cabernet Sauvignon, Zinfandel, Shiraz/Syrah, and Sangiovese are all good options. Select a bottle that is inexpensive but still good enough to drink, and always avoid "cooking wines," which contain additives.

PRO TIP

This is the kind of meal you're likely to make only as much as you need. If you'd like to make fewer steaks, that's fine, but still make the same amount of sauce (the sauce recipe does not scale down well and it's always nice to have a little extra sauce). Also, keep in mind that with fewer steaks in the pan, they'll cook a bit faster (for medium-rare, figure 3 to 4 minutes per side).

For birthday celebrations at our house, the birthday person gets to request his or her favorite dinner. My husband *always* requests filet mignon. Here, I sear the filets in a hot skillet, then build a pan sauce with shallots, red wine, and beef broth. It's simple enough to pull off on a busy weeknight, yet it tastes like dinner at a fancy steakhouse.

Serves 4

4 (6-ounce/170 g) filets mignons

Kosher salt and freshly ground black pepper

1 tablespoon vegetable oil

3 tablespoons unsalted butter, softened

¾ cup (90 g) thinly sliced shallot (from 2 large shallots)

2 garlic cloves, minced

⅔ cup (160 mL) dry red wine

1½ cups (360 mL) beef broth

½ teaspoon sugar

2 tablespoons all-purpose flour

2 teaspoons finely chopped fresh thyme

1. Pat the steaks dry, and if they are thick, gently press them down with the palm of your hand so that they are about 1½ inches (4 cm) thick. Season the steaks all over with 1 heaping teaspoon of kosher salt and ½ teaspoon of pepper.

2. In a large stainless-steel or cast-iron skillet, heat the oil over medium-high heat. When the oil is hot and shimmering, add the steaks and cook for about 4 minutes on each side, turning only once, for medium-rare (or about 5 minutes per side for medium). Transfer the steaks to a plate and tent with foil.

3. Reduce the heat to low and add 1 tablespoon of the butter to the pan. When the butter is melted, add the shallots and cook, stirring frequently, until they soften and start to brown, 2 to 3 minutes. Add the garlic and cook 1 minute more. Add the wine and bring to a boil over medium-high heat; cook, scraping the pan with a wooden spoon to release any browned bits, until the wine is reduced by about two-thirds, about 4 minutes. Add the broth, sugar, and ¼ teaspoon kosher salt; bring to a boil, then reduce the heat to medium low and simmer for 4 minutes.

4. While the sauce simmers, in a small bowl, mash the remaining 2 tablespoons softened butter with the flour to make a smooth paste.

5. Whisk half the butter-flour paste into the sauce and simmer until thickened, about 30 seconds. Whisk in more paste, little by little, until the sauce is thickened to your liking (you may not need all of it). Stir in the thyme, a few grinds of pepper, and any juice that accumulated on the plate holding the steaks. Taste and adjust the seasoning if necessary. Transfer the steaks to serving plates; spoon the sauce over and around the steaks or pass it at the table.

Dijon & Panko–Crusted Rack of Lamb

Though we think of rack of lamb as a special occasion dish because of the price, it's quick and easy enough to prepare any weeknight. This classic French preparation is the way I learned to cook it when I was an apprentice at L'Auberge Chez Francois in Great Falls, Virginia, and it's still my favorite method. The meat turns out exceptionally flavorful, especially considering how simple the recipe is.

Serves 4

2 (8-rib) lamb rib roasts (about 2 pounds/907 g each), bones frenched, meat trimmed of fat and silver skin

Salt and freshly ground black pepper

2 tablespoons plus 1 teaspoon olive oil

½ cup (30 g) panko bread crumbs

¾ teaspoon finely chopped fresh thyme, or ¼ teaspoon dried

2 tablespoons Dijon mustard

1. Preheat the oven to 400°F (205°C) and set an oven rack in the middle position.

2. Sprinkle the lamb evenly with 1 teaspoon each of salt and pepper.

3. Heat 2 tablespoons of the oil in a heavy ovenproof skillet (cast-iron or stainless-steel; see Pro Tip) over high heat. With your exhaust fan on, sear the lamb for 4 minutes on each side, or until nicely browned. Don't worry about searing the ends; they'll brown in the oven. (The bones of the racks will hang over the edges of the skillet; that's okay.)

4. Meanwhile, in a small bowl, combine the panko with the remaining teaspoon oil, the thyme, ¼ teaspoon salt, and a few grinds of black pepper. Toss until the panko is well coated with the oil and seasonings.

5. Using a spoon or brush, spread the mustard all over the meat—you can do this right in the pan (after you've removed it from the heat), using tongs to maneuver the racks—then arrange the racks fat side up in the skillet. Sprinkle the panko mixture over the mustard coating on the top and sides of the racks (don't worry about the bottom), pressing with your hands to adhere.

6. Slide the pan into the oven and roast for 15 to 18 minutes, or until a thermometer inserted into the center of one of the roasts registers between 135°F/57°C (medium) and 140°F/60°C (medium-well). (Keep in mind that these temperatures account for the fact that the temperature will continue to rise several degrees while the meat rests.) Transfer the racks to a cutting board and let rest for 10 minutes, then cut into single or double chops.

SOURCING SAVVY

The most time-consuming part of the recipe is trimming the fat and silver skin off the racks, so try to get your butcher to do it for you (there are good YouTube tutorials online if you have to do it yourself).

PRO TIPS

The USDA recommends cooking lamb to a temperature of at least 145°F/63°C, but many people prefer it rarer. I think an internal temperature of 135°F/57°C (medium) is perfect, as the meat continues to rise several degrees while resting. Cook a bit longer to meet USDA guidelines.

—

If you don't have an ovenproof skillet, transfer the racks to a foil-lined baking sheet before roasting.

Old-Fashioned Individual Meatloaves

MAKE-AHEAD/FREEZER-FRIENDLY INSTRUCTIONS

The cooked meatloaves can be made 2 days ahead and refrigerated, or frozen for up to 3 months. If frozen, defrost overnight in the refrigerator and then reheat uncovered, on a baking sheet in a 300°F (150°C) oven until hot in the middle.

PRO TIP

The trickiest part of this recipe is making the loaves of equal size. I usually divide the meat mixture roughly in half and then divide each half roughly into thirds. Then, I scoop large balls of the mixture onto the prepared baking sheet, reapportion if necessary, and shape into loaves.

This is a very good, very simple meatloaf recipe, and it's a real stick-to-your-ribber. The purpose of shaping the loaves into individual portions is twofold: first, it speeds up the cooking time, making it more doable on a weeknight (these take 40 minutes to bake rather than 70 minutes!); second, it allows more surface area for the ketchup glaze, so you can get some of the glaze in every bite. One tip if you're making this for kids: be sure to chop the onions very fine. My experience is that kids do not like finding flecks of onions (or flecks of anything, really) in their meatloaves. Naturally, leftovers make excellent meatloaf sandwiches.

Serves 6

2 tablespoons olive oil

1 large yellow onion, finely chopped

4 garlic cloves, minced

¼ cup (60 mL) milk

2 large eggs

1 teaspoon dried thyme

1 heaping teaspoon salt

½ teaspoon freshly ground black pepper

2 tablespoons Worcestershire sauce

2½ pounds (1.1 kg) meatloaf mix (see Sourcing Savvy, page 119)

¾ cup (105 g) plain bread crumbs

About ¾ cup (173 g) ketchup

1. Preheat the oven to 350°F (175°C) and set an oven rack in the middle position. Line a 13 x 18-inch (33 x 46 cm) baking sheet with parchment paper.

2. Heat the oil in a medium skillet over medium heat. Add the onion and cook, stirring frequently, until softened, about 5 minutes. Add the garlic and cook 1 minute more. Do not brown. Transfer to a large bowl.

3. To the bowl, add the milk, eggs, thyme, salt, pepper, and Worcestershire. Whisk to combine.

4. Add the meatloaf mix and bread crumbs to the egg mixture and mix with your hands until just combined.

5. Form the mixture into 6 small (9-ounce/255 g) loaves and place on the prepared baking sheet. Spoon the ketchup over the top and sides of each loaf. Bake for 40 to 45 minutes, or until an instant-read thermometer registers 160°F (71°C) in the middle of a meatloaf. Let the meatloaves rest for about 5 minutes. Scrape any fat away from the edges of each meatloaf, then use a spatula to transfer the meatloaves to a serving platter or plates.

Simple Sides

Most weeknights, I keep my side dishes super-simple so I can focus my time and creativity on the main course. These are the seven basic sides I have on repeat. They complement most entrées, and they are so easy, I can practically make them with my eyes closed.

Rice Pilaf

Serves 4 to 6

3 tablespoons unsalted butter

⅓ cup (24 g) minced shallot
(from 1 large shallot)

1½ cups (400 g) long-grain rice

3 cups (960 mL) chicken broth

Heaping ½ teaspoon salt

¼ teaspoon freshly ground
black pepper

1 bay leaf

1 sprig fresh thyme (optional)

2 tablespoons finely chopped fresh
Italian parsley (optional)

1. In a medium saucepan, melt the butter over medium heat. Add the shallot and cook, stirring frequently, until soft and translucent, 2 to 3 minutes. Do not brown. Add the rice and cook, stirring constantly, until the grains are coated with butter and slightly toasted, 2 to 3 minutes.

2. Add the broth, salt, pepper, bay leaf, and thyme (if using) and bring to a boil. Reduce the heat to a simmer, cover the pan tightly, and cook for 18 to 20 minutes, until the rice is tender and the broth is absorbed. Taste the rice; if it is not quite tender enough, add ¼ cup of water, cover, and simmer for a few minutes more.

3. Remove the pan from the heat and let stand, covered, for about 5 minutes. Taste and adjust the seasoning if necessary. Add the parsley, if using, then fluff the rice with a fork and serve.

Rustic Parmesan Mashed Potatoes

Serves 4 to 6

3 quarts (3 L) water

Salt

2 pounds (907 g) baby red
potatoes, sliced in half

6 tablespoons (¾ stick/3 ounces/
85 g) unsalted butter, cut into
tablespoons

½ cup (50 g) finely grated
Parmigiano-Reggiano cheese

½ teaspoon freshly ground
black pepper

1 tablespoon chopped fresh
chives (optional)

1. Bring the water and 2 teaspoons of salt to a boil. Boil the potatoes until fork-tender, 20 to 25 minutes.

2. Use a slotted spoon or handheld strainer to transfer the potatoes to a shallow bowl; reserve the cooking water. Top the potatoes with the butter, Parmigiano-Reggiano, ¾ teaspoon salt, and the pepper. Use a fork to smash the potatoes, adding hot cooking liquid as necessary to make the potatoes as creamy as you like (I usually add about ½ cup/120 mL). Taste and adjust the seasoning if necessary. Sprinkle fresh chives over the top, if using, and serve.

Perfect Couscous

Serves 4 to 6

1¾ cups (420 mL) low-sodium chicken broth or water

½ teaspoon salt

1 tablespoon unsalted butter

1 tablespoon extra-virgin olive oil

1½ cups (10 ounces/113 g) couscous

In a medium saucepan, bring the broth, salt, butter, and oil to a boil. Stir in the couscous, cover with a tight-fitting lid, and remove from the heat. Let the couscous steam for 5 minutes. Use a fork to fluff the couscous and break up any clumps. Serve warm.

Roasted Broccoli

PRO TIP
When roasting vegetables, make sure they are all cut roughly the same size to ensure even cooking. Also, dry them well before tossing with oil and seasonings; you don't want them to steam in the oven. Finally, don't crowd the pan; if you want to increase the recipe, use two baking sheets.

Serves 4 to 6

1½ pounds (680 g) broccoli crowns, cut into 2-inch (5 cm) florets

3 tablespoons extra-virgin olive oil

½ teaspoon salt

¼ teaspoon freshly ground black pepper

1. Preheat the oven to 450°F (220°C) and set an oven rack in the middle position. Line a baking sheet with heavy-duty aluminum foil.

2. Directly on the prepared baking sheet, using your hands or a rubber spatula, toss the broccoli with the oil, salt, and pepper. Spread into a single layer and roast for 13 to 15 minutes, until the broccoli is crisp-tender and caramelized on the bottom. Taste and adjust seasoning if necessary.

Roasted Brussels Sprouts

Serves 4 to 6

1½ pounds (680 g) Brussels sprouts, stems and ragged outer leaves removed, halved

3 tablespoons extra-virgin olive oil

½ teaspoon salt

¼ teaspoon freshly ground black pepper

1. Preheat the oven to 425°F (220°C) and set an oven rack in the middle position. Line a baking sheet with heavy-duty aluminum foil.

2. Directly on the prepared baking sheet, using your hands or a rubber spatula, toss the Brussels sprouts with the oil, salt, and pepper. Spread into a single layer and roast, stirring once halfway through, until the Brussels sprouts are crisp-tender and golden brown, 18 to 20 minutes. Taste and adjust the seasoning, if necessary, and serve.

Roasted Carrots

Serves 4 to 6

2 pounds carrots (907 g), peeled and sliced on the diagonal about 2 inches (5 cm) thick

2 tablespoons extra-virgin olive oil

½ teaspoon salt

¼ teaspoon freshly ground black pepper

2 teaspoons chopped fresh thyme, or ½ teaspoon dried

1. Preheat the oven to 425°F (220°C) and set an oven rack in the middle position. Line a 13 x 18-inch (33 x 46 cm) baking sheet with heavy-duty aluminum foil.

2. Directly on the prepared baking sheet, using your hands or a rubber spatula, toss the carrots with the oil, salt, pepper, and thyme. Roast, stirring once halfway through, until nicely caramelized and tender, 20 to 25 minutes. Taste and adjust the seasoning if necessary.

Roasted Asparagus

Serves 4

1 bunch of asparagus (about 1 pound/454 g), tough ends trimmed

2 tablespoons extra-virgin olive oil

¼ teaspoon salt

¼ teaspoon freshly ground black pepper

1. Preheat the oven to 425°F (220°C) and set an oven rack in the middle position. Line a 13 x 18-inch (33 x 46 cm) baking sheet with heavy-duty aluminum foil.

2. Spread the asparagus in a single layer on the prepared baking sheet. Drizzle with the oil and sprinkle with the salt and pepper. Shake the pan to coat the asparagus evenly.

3. Roast the asparagus until crisp-tender, 6 to 8 minutes, depending on thickness.

Something Sweet

Brownie Pudding

Think of this fudgy chocolate dessert as a family-style molten lava cake. It is brownie-like around the edges and gooey in the center. I've given a range for the baking time, depending on how lava-like you'd like the center to be. For me, 18 minutes is just right, but everyone's oven is a bit different. Be sure to serve this immediately after cooling; it will continue cooking as it sits (not a bad thing . . . just less lava!).

Serves 6 to 8

½ cup (1 stick/4 ounces/113 g) unsalted butter, plus more for greasing the pan

6 ounces (170 g) best-quality bittersweet chocolate, chopped

2 large eggs

2 large egg yolks

⅔ cup (144 g) light brown sugar

1 teaspoon vanilla extract

Pinch of salt

⅓ cup (43 g) all-purpose flour

Vanilla ice cream or Sweetened Whipped Cream (page 261), for serving

1. Preheat the oven to 350°F (175°C) and set an oven rack in the middle position. Generously butter a 2-quart (2 L) baking dish.

2. Melt the butter in a medium bowl in the microwave. Immediately add the chocolate and stir until the chocolate is completely melted and smooth. If a few chunks remain, place the bowl back in the microwave for 15 to 20 seconds, then stir again.

3. In the bowl of an electric mixer fitted with the paddle attachment or beaters, beat the eggs, egg yolks, brown sugar, vanilla, and salt (on medium-high speed if using a stand mixer, high speed if using a handheld mixer), about 4 minutes. Fold in the melted chocolate mixture and the flour until just combined (the chocolate sinks to the bottom, so be sure to scrape it up into the batter).

4. Pour the batter into the prepared baking dish and smooth the top. Bake for 17 to 20 minutes, depending on how molten you'd like it (17 minutes for molten, 20 minutes for more cake-like). Let the pudding cool for about 5 minutes, then spoon it into bowls and serve it warm with vanilla ice cream or whipped cream. (The pudding is best enjoyed warm from the oven, but leftovers can be covered with foil and stored at room temperature for up to 3 days.)

Chocolate Chip Skillet Cookie

Making chocolate chip cookie dough is easy—I believe I started whipping up my own (mostly to eat raw) with my girlfriends in the fifth grade. Cooking the dough in a skillet is not only way more fun than making individual cookies, but it's also faster because you don't have to roll the dough into balls. You can slice this skillet cookie into wedges, but if it's just family, plunk a few scoops of vanilla or coffee ice cream in the center, place the skillet on the table, hand out spoons, and let everyone dig in. It will be gooey, like a fresh-out-of-the-oven chocolate chip cookie. If you'd like it firmer, you'll need to let it cool a bit longer, about 45 minutes—if you can wait that long!

Serves 8 to 10

¾ cup (1½ sticks/6 ounces/170g) unsalted butter, at room temperature

½ cup (100 g) granulated sugar

⅔ cup (155 g) packed dark brown sugar

1 teaspoon vanilla extract

1 large egg

1 large egg yolk

1 teaspoon salt

½ teaspoon baking powder

¼ teaspoon baking soda

1½ cups (173 g) all-purpose flour

Scant 1 cup (170 g) semisweet chocolate chips

Vanilla or coffee ice cream, for serving

MAKE-AHEAD/FREEZER-FRIENDLY INSTRUCTIONS

The dough can be refrigerated, wrapped tightly in plastic, for up to 1 week or frozen for up to 1 month.

PRO TIP

If you don't have a 10-inch (25 cm) cast-iron skillet, an oven-safe nonstick skillet will work, too, but be careful not to scratch the surface when slicing. You could also use a stainless-steel pan lined with parchment paper or a 2-quart (2 L) baking dish. (With any of these options, start checking for doneness around 27 minutes, as the cookie will bake a bit faster.)

1. Preheat the oven to 350°F (175°C) and set a rack in the middle position.

2. In the bowl of an electric mixer fitted with the paddle attachment or beaters, beat the butter and both sugars for 3 minutes, until light and fluffy. Scrape down the sides and bottom of the bowl as necessary. Beat in the vanilla, egg, and egg yolk, and then beat for 2 minutes more. Scrape down the bowl. Add the salt, baking powder, and baking soda and beat briefly to combine. Add the flour and mix to combine. Reserve a few tablespoons of the chocolate chips and add the rest to the batter. Mix on low speed until the chocolate is evenly distributed throughout the dough.

3. Using a spatula, spread the dough evenly in an ungreased 10-inch (25 cm) cast-iron skillet (see Pro Tip). Sprinkle the reserved chocolate chips over the top. Bake for 33 to 37 minutes, until puffed and golden. Immediately place an oven mitt over the handle of the skillet to remind yourself that it is hot (it's easy to forget, and it stays hot long after the cookie has cooled). Let cool in the skillet on a rack for 15 to 30 minutes, depending on how gooey you'd like it.

4. Slice the cookie into wedges and serve with ice cream. Cover any leftovers with aluminum foil and store at room temperature for up to 3 days.

Cherry Ricotta Cake

A riff on a lovely raspberry ricotta cake featured in *Bon Appétit* magazine years ago, this is an easy cake that you can throw together for last-minute company, so long as you have a bag of cherries in the freezer and a tub of ricotta in the fridge (the rest of the ingredients are kitchen staples). The cake comes together with two bowls and a whisk, so while it does take nearly an hour to bake, you can throw it together in minutes. Though there is a lot of ricotta in the cake, it does not taste like an Italian cheesecake; rather, it is like an ultra-moist butter cake. I love the addition of orange zest, as cherries pair beautifully with oranges, but feel free to use lemon zest instead, if that's what you have on hand. This cake is best served fresh from the oven, when the interior is still warm and the sugared top is nice and crisp.

Serves 8 to 10

Nonstick cooking spray with flour, such as Baker's Joy or Pam Baking

1½ cups (195 g) all-purpose flour

1 cup plus 2 tablespoons (225 g) sugar

2 teaspoons baking powder

½ teaspoon salt

3 large eggs

1½ cups (360 g) whole-milk ricotta

1 teaspoon vanilla extract

1½ teaspoons (packed) grated orange zest (from 1 orange)

½ cup (1 stick/4 ounces/113 g) unsalted butter, melted and slightly cooled

1⅓ cups (180 g) frozen sweet cherries (do not thaw)

1. Preheat the oven to 350° (175°C) and set an oven rack in the middle position. Spray a 9-inch (23 cm) springform pan with nonstick cooking spray with flour (alternatively, spray with nonstick cooking spray and dust with flour).

2. In a large bowl, whisk together the flour, 1 cup (200 g) of the sugar, the baking powder, and the salt.

3. In a medium bowl, whisk together the eggs, ricotta, vanilla, and orange zest. Gradually add the melted butter, whisking constantly, until evenly combined. Add the wet mixture to the dry ingredients and fold with a rubber spatula until just blended. Quickly fold in 1 cup (135 g) of the cherries; don't overmix or the cherries will bleed and turn the batter pink. Scrape the batter into the prepared pan and scatter the remaining ⅓ cup (45g) cherries over the top. Sprinkle evenly with the remaining 2 tablespoons sugar.

4. Bake the cake until golden brown and a tester inserted into the center comes out clean, 45 to 55 minutes. Let the cake cool in the pan on a rack for about 30 minutes, then remove the sides of the pan. Serve warm or at room temperature. (The cake will keep nicely for 2 to 3 days, under a cake dome or covered with foil at room temperature. Leftover slices can be toasted or reheated in a 350°F [175°C] oven until warm, about 10 minutes.)

Malted Milkshakes

Malted milkshakes became popular in the early twentieth century, when drugstores had soda fountains that served as gathering spots during Prohibition. (When people couldn't drink alcohol in bars, they enjoyed soft drinks and ice cream at soda fountains.) Legend has it that in 1922, a Chicago Walgreens employee created the malted milkshake by adding vanilla ice cream to their usual malted milk drink, a blend of milk, chocolate syrup, and malted milk powder. Over time, these milkshakes became wildly popular at soda fountains everywhere. Malted milk powder is made from malted barley extract, wheat flour, and powdered milk. It adds a savory, buttery, toasty flavor to milkshakes—and I add a pinch of salt to bring out that malted flavor even more. My kids are obsessed with these!

Makes 2 large or 4 small milkshakes

¼ cup (60 mL) milk

½ cup (65 g) malted milk powder

3 tablespoons chocolate syrup

Pinch of salt

1 quart (1 L) best-quality vanilla ice cream, such as Häagen-Dazs

In a blender, combine the milk, malted milk powder, chocolate syrup, and salt. Blend until smooth. Add the ice cream and blend just until smooth and creamy. Do not overmix or the milkshake will get thin. Pour into glasses and serve immediately.

PRO TIP

Make sure your ice cream is not too cold; it should be about the temperature it is when you get home from the supermarket, after it's been out of the freezer for a bit. I usually soften the ice cream in the microwave for 15 to 30 seconds. That way you won't have to add too much milk, and you'll have a nice thick shake.

French Apple Cake

I once worked as an au pair in Paris for a family with three little boys. My host mother, Valérie, loved to cook and would frequently enlist my help in the kitchen once the kids were in bed. Her French apple cake is a longtime favorite of mine, and it's also the most popular dessert on my website. With chunks of tart apples nestled in a tender, buttery rum cake, it is the essence of simplicity, like so many homemade French desserts.

Serves 6 to 8

1 cup (130 g) all-purpose flour

1 teaspoon baking powder

¼ teaspoon salt

½ cup (1 stick/4 ounces/113 g) unsalted butter, at room temperature

⅔ cup (133 g) granulated sugar, plus more for sprinkling

2 large eggs

1 teaspoon vanilla extract

3 tablespoons dark rum

2 large baking apples, peeled, cored, and cut into ½-inch (13 mm) cubes (see Sourcing Savvy)

Confectioners' sugar, for dusting

1. Preheat the oven to 350°F (175°C) and set an oven rack in the middle position. Grease a 9-inch (23 cm) springform or regular cake pan with butter or nonstick cooking spray. If using a regular cake pan, line the bottom of the pan with parchment paper and grease again.

2. In a small bowl, whisk together the flour, baking powder, and salt.

3. In the bowl of an electric mixer fitted with the paddle attachment or beaters, cream the butter and granulated sugar on medium speed (or medium-high speed, if using a handheld mixer) until light and fluffy, about 3 minutes. Add the eggs, one at a time, beating well and scraping down the sides of the bowl after each addition. Beat in the vanilla and rum. Don't worry if the batter looks grainy at this point; that's okay. Add the flour mixture and mix on low speed until just combined. Using a rubber spatula, fold in the apples.

4. Scrape the batter into the prepared pan and even out the top with a spatula. Sprinkle evenly with about 1 tablespoon of granulated sugar. Bake for about 40 minutes, or until the cake is golden and a toothpick inserted into the center comes out clean. Allow the cake to cool on a wire rack.

5. Run a blunt knife around the edges of the cake. If using a springform pan, remove the sides. If using a regular cake pan, carefully invert the cake onto the rack, remove the parchment paper, then gently flip the cake over and place right side up on a platter. Using a fine-mesh sieve, dust the cake with confectioners' sugar. The cake can be served warm or at room temperature, plain or with Sweetened Whipped Cream (page 261) or vanilla ice cream. (The cake keeps nicely for 2 to 3 days, under a cake dome or covered with foil at room temperature.)

Chewy, Gooey Golden Rice Krispies Treats

The inspiration for these fun treats comes from the bakery bar at Summer House Santa Monica in Bethesda, Maryland. They're made with a secret ingredient that gives the bars a distinctly toasty, caramel flavor. After one bite, you'll pause and wonder, *What's in these?* A clue? It starts with "golden" and ends with "grahams."

Makes 18 to 24 treats

1 cup (2 sticks/8 ounces/226 g) unsalted butter, plus more for buttering the pan

2 (10-ounce/284 g) bags mini marshmallows

3 cups (120 g) Golden Grahams cereal

¾ teaspoon vanilla extract

Heaping ½ teaspoon salt

5½ cups (154 g) Rice Krispies or crispy rice cereal

1. Line a 9 x 13-inch (23 x 33 cm) baking dish with heavy-duty aluminum foil, leaving 2 inches (5 cm) of overhang, and lightly grease it with softened butter or nonstick cooking spray. Set aside 2 cups of the marshmallows.

2. Place the Golden Grahams in a resealable freezer bag. Using a rolling pin, the bottom of a dry measuring cup, or your fist, pound the cereal into smaller pieces. Don't pulverize it—some pieces should be Rice Krispies–size, some should be larger, and some should be crumbs.

3. In a large pot, melt the butter over medium-high heat (save a wrapper for pressing the mixture into the pan). After the butter melts, it will begin to bubble, foam, and turn golden. Swirl or stir the butter as it continues to brown; eventually it will turn a dark golden color and smell nutty—watch carefully, as it will go from golden brown to burnt quickly. (You'll see bits of brown sediment forming; that's okay.) This whole process should take just a few minutes. Once the butter is browned, immediately remove the pan from the heat and add the remaining marshmallows, the vanilla, and salt.

4. Place the pot over low heat and stir the mixture with a wooden spoon until the marshmallows are completely melted. Remove the pot from the heat and add the crushed Golden Grahams and the Rice Krispies. Using a rubber spatula or wooden spoon, stir until evenly combined. Add the reserved marshmallows and stir until they are softened and partially melted (don't let them melt completely; you want pockets of goo). Transfer the mixture to the prepared baking dish and, using the butter wrapper or damp fingers, gently press the mixture into an even layer. Let cool at room temperature for at least 1 hour.

5. Use the foil overhang to lift the treats onto a cutting board, then use a sharp knife to cut them into 18 to 24 bars, depending on how large you'd like them.

MAKE-AHEAD/FREEZER-FRIENDLY INSTRUCTIONS

These can be made up to 2 days ahead of time and stored in an airtight container on the counter, or frozen for up to 6 weeks. To freeze, place the bars in layers separated by wax paper in an airtight container. Let stand at room temperature for a few hours before serving.

PRO TIP

When you transfer the cereal/marshmallow mixture to the pan, press it down using only light pressure to spread it out evenly. If you pack it down using too much pressure, the bars will be hard.

Raspberry Frozen Yogurt

PRO TIPS

You won't taste the vodka; it's just there to keep the yogurt creamy and smooth in the freezer. It's okay to leave it out, but you'll need to let the frozen yogurt sit out at room temperature for a bit before scooping.

—

The most efficient way to strain out the seeds is to set a fine-mesh sieve over a bowl, pour the yogurt mixture in, and then use a ladle to push the mixture in circular motions through the sieve.

This frozen yogurt tastes intensely of fresh raspberries, almost a cross between frozen yogurt and sorbet—and the color is such fun! It takes only a few minutes to whip up in a blender (although count on at least 15 to 20 minutes for it to freeze in your ice cream machine), and it's the perfect semi-healthy treat to have on hand when you just need a few spoonfuls of something sweet after dinner.

For the best taste and consistency, use whole-milk Greek yogurt. And opt for frozen raspberries over fresh. I don't know the science behind it, but the yogurt ends up with a more vibrant flavor and color using frozen fruit (bonus: frozen raspberries are less expensive than fresh). You'll need a 2-quart (2 L) ice cream machine to freeze all the mixture at once. If you have a smaller machine, you can cut the recipe in half or freeze the mixture in two batches.

Serves 6

2 (10-ounce/283 g) bags frozen raspberries, thawed, with their juices

2¼ cups (540 g) plain whole-milk Greek yogurt

2 tablespoons vodka (see Pro Tip)

1½ cups (300 g) sugar

1. Combine the raspberries, yogurt, vodka, and sugar in a blender. Blend until completely smooth. To strain the seeds, pass the mixture through a fine-mesh sieve into a bowl (see Pro Tip). Discard the seeds.

2. Freeze the yogurt mixture in an ice cream maker according to the manufacturer's instructions. Serve the frozen yogurt soft serve–style directly from the ice cream maker or transfer to a plastic container and place in the freezer for a few hours, until firm enough to scoop. Allow the yogurt to sit out at room temperature for about 10 minutes before scooping.

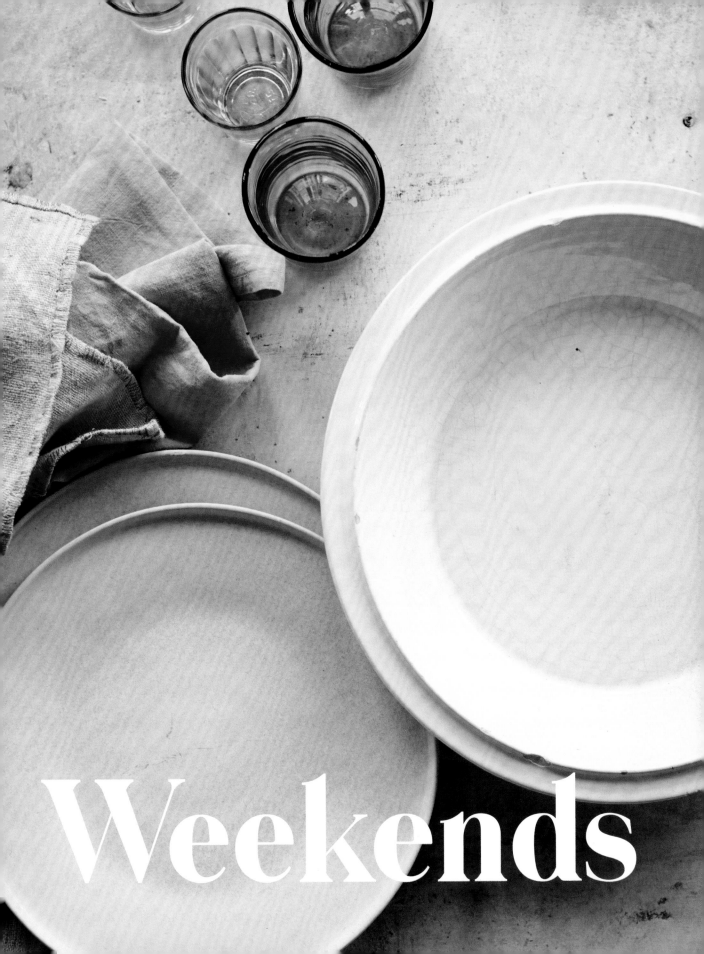

Weekends

My mother always says,

"However you are when you're young, you just get 'more so' as you get older."

It's true: I have always been a homebody, and the older I get, the more I love being at home, especially in the kitchen. On the weekends, my husband is out the door at the crack of dawn to play golf or tennis. I, on the other hand, roll out of bed and turn on the oven even before I brew my coffee or decide what I'm going to cook.

Whether I'm baking something for my kids or working on a recipe for my blog, the kitchen is my favorite place to be. Being creative, working with my hands, focusing on the steps of a recipe, filling the house with delicious aromas—all these calm my mind and make me happy. Even thinking about food is fun for me. I love sitting on the back porch and losing myself in a good cookbook, escaping into someone else's kitchen, and dreaming up what I'll cook next. It doesn't hurt that cooking is practical, too; there's always something delicious to eat and share in the end!

These chapters are filled with some of my favorite leisurely recipes, for when you have a few hours to putter around the kitchen. There are pancakes and scones and popovers that will rouse your sleepy family out of bed; company-for-brunch recipes, including a coffee cake that tempts you to "even out the pan" every time you walk by; slow-cooking roasts and stews that make you grateful for cold and dreary weather; festive dinners to share with family and friends; and finally, over-the-top desserts for holidays, special occasions, or "just because."

Leisurely Brunch

Cucumber Gin Lemonade

I was so proud of myself after creating this summery cocktail, but then I went online and realized it was already very much a thing. Oh well, I guess it just proves the old adage: Everything worth doing has already been done. Lemonade and gin are a classic combination, but the addition of cucumber slices gives the drink a refreshing, spa-like twist—perfect for sipping on the patio on a warm day. Feel free to play around with the level of alcohol to suit your taste. My husband always adds an extra pour of gin to his drink, but it's good even without the gin.

PRO TIP

Wait to add the ice until pouring the drink into glasses; if you add ice to the bowl, it will melt and dilute the flavor of the drink.

Serves 4

1 cup (240 mL) fresh lemon juice, strained (from 5 lemons)

1 lemon, thinly sliced into rounds, seeded

⅔ cup (160 mL) gin

½ English/hothouse cucumber, thinly sliced into rounds

⅓ cup (67 g) sugar

1½ cups (360 mL) water

Ice, for serving

½ cup (8 g) fresh mint leaves, for serving

1. In a medium bowl, combine the lemon juice, lemon slices, gin, cucumber, sugar, and water. Stir until the sugar is dissolved. Taste and adjust with more gin, sugar, or lemon juice, if necessary. Cover with plastic wrap and refrigerate for at least 1 hour or overnight.

2. Fill highball glasses with ice and mint leaves, and ladle the drink, along with the cucumber and lemon slices, over the top.

Nut & Dried Fruit Bars

PRO TIP

Because of the way it's packaged, parchment paper has a tendency to roll up when you attempt to line a pan with it. It's pesky but easy to fix. Put a little dot of butter in each corner of the pan. The butter will act as a glue to hold the parchment in place.

Filled with sticky maple-glazed nuts and dried fruit, these bars remind me of KIND bars, only better! In fact, my husband, Michael, calls them "breakfast candy bars" because they are so delicious and rich.

Makes 12 bars

1½ tablespoons cornstarch

½ cup (120 mL) maple syrup

Scant ¾ teaspoon salt

2⅓ cups (327 g) unsalted mixed nuts (any combination), very coarsely chopped

⅓ cup (47 g) dried cranberries

3 tablespoons dried blueberries

1. Line an 8-inch (20 cm) square baking dish with parchment paper, leaving a slight overhang.

2. Put the cornstarch in a small bowl. Add a few tablespoons of the maple syrup and whisk until smooth, and then gradually whisk in the remaining maple syrup and salt.

3. In a medium (10-inch/25 cm) nonstick skillet, stir together the maple mixture and the nuts. Cook over medium heat, stirring frequently with a wooden spoon, until the syrup is completely absorbed by the nuts, the nuts are a bit sticky, and the light-colored nuts are just starting to turn golden, 7 to 9 minutes. Remove the pan from the heat and mix in the dried cranberries and blueberries.

4. Pour the mixture into the prepared pan; using a spatula, press the sticky mixture firmly into a compact, even layer. If the nuts are too sticky to press with the spatula, place a piece of parchment paper over the nuts and press them flat with your hand (careful—the mixture is hot). Let cool until just set and still slightly warm, about 20 minutes (no longer, as the bars are harder to cut when completely cool).

5. Using the parchment overhang, lift the unsliced bars out of the pan and lay them on a cutting board (the parchment will remain under the bars while you slice them). Using a sharp knife, slice into bars (they will be slightly sticky when you cut them—that's normal). Let the bars cool completely, then store them in a single layer in a covered container lined with parchment at room temperature for up to a week. (If you don't have a large enough container, layer the bars between parchment.)

Buttermilk Pancakes

Whenever I have a carton of buttermilk to use up, I make these fluffy buttermilk pancakes with crispy edges. They're a delicious way to get sleepy kids out of bed in the morning on the right foot. In fact, one of my recipe testers told me that her kids, ages five and three, rated the pancakes a "thumbs double," which is their highest rating—higher than a simple "thumbs-up." How cute is that? If you'd like to add chocolate chips or blueberries, simply dot them over the raw pancakes immediately after ladling the batter onto the griddle.

Serves 4 to 6 (makes 16 medium pancakes)

2 cups (260 g) all-purpose flour

2 tablespoons sugar

1 tablespoon baking powder

½ teaspoon baking soda

1 teaspoon salt

2 large eggs

2¼ cups (540 mL) buttermilk

4 tablespoons (½ stick/2 ounces/ 56 g) unsalted butter, melted and slightly cooled

Vegetable oil, for cooking

Maple syrup, for serving

1. Combine the flour, sugar, baking powder, baking soda, and salt in a large bowl and mix well.

2. Beat the eggs in a medium bowl. Whisk in the buttermilk and melted butter.

3. Pour the buttermilk mixture into the bowl with the dry ingredients and whisk until all of the dry ingredients are moistened. Do not overmix; the batter should look a little lumpy. (Note that the batter will be quite thick; as it sits, the leavening will activate and create air bubbles.)

4. Heat a griddle or nonstick pan over medium-low heat and coat it with vegetable oil. Drop the batter from a ladle or large spoon (about ¼ cup/ 60 mL per pancake) and cook until the first side is golden brown, or until the surface bubbles and is dotted with holes, about 2 minutes. Flip and cook on the other side until golden brown; this happens quickly, so peek after 30 seconds. Wipe the griddle clean with paper towels, add more oil, and repeat with the remaining batter, adjusting the heat as necessary. Serve immediately with maple syrup.

FREEZER-FRIENDLY INSTRUCTIONS

The pancakes can be frozen for up to 3 months. To freeze, let the pancakes cool completely, then stack the pancakes with a sheet of parchment or wax paper between each. Wrap the stack tightly in aluminum foil or place it inside a resealable freezer bag. To reheat, place the pancakes in a single layer on a 13 x 18-inch (33 x 46 cm) baking sheet and cover with foil. Bake in a 375°F (190°C) oven for 8 to 10 minutes, or until hot.

Cranberry, Orange & Walnut Cream Scones

MAKE-AHEAD/FREEZER-FRIENDLY INSTRUCTIONS

The dough can be made, shaped, and refrigerated overnight, or frozen for up to 3 months. If refrigerated, bake the scones directly from the refrigerator as directed. To freeze, place the dough wedges on a 13 x 18-inch (33 x 46 cm) baking sheet, let set in the freezer, then place in a resealable freezer bag and press out as much air as possible. Bake as needed directly from the freezer. (Allow 1 to 2 minutes longer in the oven.)

Sweet, orange-scented, and studded with dried fruit and nuts, these scones practically scream holidays. They are buttery, tender, and flaky, much like a biscuit—a far cry from all those dry and crumbly coffee shop scones. The secret is replacing some of the flour in the dough with cornstarch, which gives the scones a lighter texture. If you want to mix things up, swap out the cranberries and walnuts for dried cherries and pecans. These are generous scones; feel free to cut them a bit smaller to increase the yield.

Makes 8 scones

FOR THE SCONES

1¾ cups (228 g) all-purpose flour, plus more for dusting

3 tablespoons cornstarch

¾ teaspoon salt

1 tablespoon baking powder

¼ cup (50 g) granulated sugar

7 tablespoons (99 g) cold unsalted butter, cut into ¼-inch (6 mm) pieces

⅔ cup (93 g) dried cranberries

½ cup (60 g) walnuts, chopped (toasted, if desired; see page 204)

1 large egg

⅔ cup (160 mL) heavy cream

1 teaspoon vanilla extract

1 teaspoon grated orange zest (from 1 orange)

FOR THE GLAZE

1 cup (116 g) confectioners' sugar

⅛ teaspoon grated orange zest

1 to 2 tablespoons fresh orange juice (from 1 orange)

1. Preheat the oven to 425°F (220°C) and set an oven rack in the middle position. Line a 13 x 18-inch (33 x 46 cm) baking sheet with parchment paper.

2. Make the scones: In a large bowl, whisk together the flour, cornstarch, salt, baking powder, and granulated sugar. Add the butter and use your fingers to rub it into the dry ingredients until the mixture resembles coarse meal with pea-sized clumps of butter within. Stir in the cranberries and walnuts.

3. In a small bowl, whisk together the egg, cream, vanilla, and orange zest. Add to the flour mixture and stir just until the dough comes together into a slightly sticky, clumpy mass.

-RECIPE CONTINUES-

4. Dust a clean work surface lightly with flour and place the dough on top; dust the dough lightly with flour as well. Using a light hand, knead the dough gently a few times until it comes together into a ball; sprinkle with more flour, as necessary, if it is too sticky to work with. Press the dough into a flat circle about ¾ inch (2 cm) high; using a sharp knife, cut into 8 triangles.

5. Transfer the wedges to the prepared baking sheet, spacing them about 2 inches (5 cm) apart. Bake for 11 to 14 minutes, until the tops are very lightly golden and firm to the touch. Let the scones cool on the baking sheet for a few minutes, then transfer them to a wire rack to cool completely.

6. Make the glaze: In a small bowl, whisk together the confectioners' sugar, orange zest, and 1 tablespoon orange juice. Gradually add more orange juice as needed until the glaze is the consistency of thick glue.

7. Drizzle the glaze over the cooled scones and let it set before serving. The scones are best served fresh, the day they are baked.

HOW TO TOAST WALNUTS

Preheat the oven to 350°F (175°C) and set an oven rack in the middle position. Arrange the walnuts in a single layer on a baking sheet. Bake, checking frequently, until lightly toasted and fragrant, 6 to 8 minutes. Immediately transfer the walnuts to a plate and let cool.

Old-Fashioned Cinnamon Swirl Crumb Cake

I created this recipe for my daughter, Anna, who adores the cinnamon coffee cake from a certain popular coffeehouse chain. It has a sweet cinnamon swirl running through the center, a generous crumb topping, and a wonderful flavor from the addition of ground nutmeg and buttermilk. Pair a slice of this cake with a mug of warm apple cider and you're all set for fall.

Makes one 9 x 13-inch (23 x 33 cm) cake • Serves 12 to 16

Nonstick cooking spray

FOR THE CRUMB TOPPING

½ cup (1 stick/4 ounces/113 g) unsalted butter, melted

½ cup (100 g) granulated sugar

½ cup (116 g) packed dark brown sugar

1 tablespoon ground cinnamon

Heaping ¼ teaspoon salt

1⅓ cups (173 g) all-purpose flour

2 tablespoons cornstarch

FOR THE CINNAMON SWIRL

⅔ cup (58 g) packed dark brown sugar

1 tablespoon ground cinnamon

FOR THE CAKE

3 cups (390 g) all-purpose flour

1½ teaspoons baking powder

¾ teaspoon baking soda

¾ teaspoon salt

Heaping ½ teaspoon ground nutmeg

¾ cup (1½ sticks/6 ounces/170 g) unsalted butter, at room temperature

1½ cups (300 g) granulated sugar

4 large eggs

1½ teaspoons vanilla extract

1¼ cups (300 mL) buttermilk

HEADS UP

This cake is really big! If you'd like to halve the recipe, use an 8-inch (20 cm) square pan; the baking time will be 45 to 50 minutes.

MAKE-AHEAD/FREEZER-FRIENDLY INSTRUCTIONS

The cake keeps well for several days covered tightly with foil and stored at room temperature. It can also be tightly wrapped in foil and stored in an airtight container in the freezer for up to 3 months. Thaw overnight at room temperature.

1. Preheat the oven to 325°F (165°C) and set an oven rack in the middle position. Spray a 9 x 13-inch (23 x 33 cm) ceramic, glass, or pale metal baking pan with nonstick cooking spray.

2. Make the crumb topping: In a medium bowl, stir together the melted butter, granulated sugar, brown sugar, cinnamon, and salt. Add the flour and cornstarch and mix until mostly absorbed by the butter mixture. Finish mixing with your hands until evenly combined and the mixture is a blend of crumbs and chickpea-size clumps.

3. Make the cinnamon swirl: In a small bowl, using your fingers, mix the brown sugar and cinnamon until evenly combined.

-RECIPE CONTINUES-

4. Make the cake: In a medium bowl, whisk together the flour, baking powder, baking soda, salt, and nutmeg. Set aside.

5. In the bowl of a stand mixer fitted with the paddle attachment or beaters, beat the butter and granulated sugar on medium speed until evenly moistened, about 1 minute. Scrape down the sides of the bowl, then add the eggs one at a time, beating to incorporate after each addition, and scraping the bowl as necessary (don't worry if the mixture looks a bit curdled at any point; it will smooth out in the end). Continue beating on medium speed (or medium-high speed if using a handheld mixer) for about 3 minutes, until pale and creamy. Beat in the vanilla. With the mixer on low speed, beat in one-fourth of the flour mixture, then one-third of the buttermilk. Beat in another fourth of the flour, then another third of the buttermilk. Repeat with another fourth of the flour and the remaining buttermilk mixture. Finally, beat in the remaining flour mixture. Scrape down the sides and bottom of the bowl, and briefly mix by hand to make sure all of the ingredients are well incorporated and the batter is smooth.

6. Scrape about half the batter into the prepared pan (it will only come about ⅓ inch/8 mm up the sides of the pan). Sprinkle the cinnamon swirl mixture evenly over the top. Using a soup spoon, dollop the remaining batter evenly over the cinnamon mixture. You don't need to spread it out; it's okay if the cinnamon mixture peeks through in spots. Using a butter knife, swirl the layers by making about 6 figure-eights around the pan. Don't overdo the swirling!

7. Starting around the edges and working your way in, sprinkle the crumb topping mixture evenly over the top. (It may seem like a lot of crumbs in proportion to the batter, but it all balances out when the cake bakes.)

8. Bake for 45 to 55 minutes, or until the cake is golden around the edges, the topping is slightly browned, and a cake tester comes out clean. Let the cake cool on a rack for at least 1 hour; serve warm or at room temperature.

Coconut Biscotti

FREEZER-FRIENDLY INSTRUCTIONS

The biscotti can be double-wrapped in aluminum foil or plastic freezer wrap and frozen for up to 3 months. Thaw overnight on the countertop before serving.

SOURCING SAVVY

Unsweetened shredded coconut is finely shredded coconut with most of the moisture removed. Since it gets pulverized in the recipe, you might wonder if you can replace it with coconut flour. You can't. The two are not interchangeable, as coconut flour has the moisture *and* fat removed, making it drier.

——

There are two kinds of coconut oil: virgin (or extra-virgin) and refined. Virgin coconut oil is less processed than the refined version, giving it a more pronounced coconut flavor. All coconut oil is solid at room temperature, and depending on how warm your room is, the oil may be solid or liquidy.

Sweet but not cloying, crunchy but not tooth-shattering, these are lovely biscotti. They have a subtle coconut flavor that sort of sneaks up on you as you eat them, and the flavor gets more "coconuty" with every bite. Don't skip the sparkling sugar on top—you'll love the festive shimmer and extra crunch it adds. Serve the cookies with coffee or tea any time of day, and pace yourself—they are so light I could eat a dozen of them without even thinking about it! These biscotti are sturdy and keep well for up to two weeks, so they are ideal for gift-giving or sending away to friends and relatives.

Makes 32 biscotti

1½ cups (195 g) all-purpose flour, plus more for dusting

1 cup (80 g) finely shredded unsweetened coconut

1½ teaspoons baking powder

¾ teaspoon salt

¼ cup plus 2 tablespoons (83 g) virgin coconut oil, at room temperature (but not liquid; see Sourcing Savvy)

⅔ cup (133 g) granulated sugar

2 teaspoons vanilla extract

2 large eggs

2 teaspoons white sparkling sugar, for sprinkling

1. In the bowl of a food processor, combine the flour, shredded coconut, baking powder, and salt. Process until the coconut is finely ground and powdery, about 1 minute.

2. In the bowl of an electric mixer fitted with the paddle attachment or beaters, cream the coconut oil, granulated sugar, and vanilla on medium speed until light and creamy, about 1 minute. Add the eggs, one at a time, beating well after each addition, and scraping down the bowl as necessary. Add the flour-coconut mixture and mix on low speed until just combined.

3. Scrape the dough onto a piece of plastic wrap; wrap and chill in the refrigerator until firm enough to handle, about 40 minutes.

4. Preheat the oven to 350°F (175°C) and set an oven rack in the middle position. Line a 13 x 18-inch (33 x 46 cm) baking sheet with parchment paper.

5. Unwrap the chilled dough and cut it in half. Dust your hands lightly with flour and, working directly on the lined baking sheet, form each portion into a long rectangle 1½ inches (4 cm) wide x 12 inches (30 cm) long x ¾ inch (2 cm) tall. (If the dough is sticky, dust your hands with more flour as necessary.) Leave about 4 inches (10 cm) of space between the logs to allow the dough to spread.

6. Sprinkle the logs with the sparkling sugar. Bake for 20 to 23 minutes, rotating the pan from front to back midway through, until firm to the touch and golden around the bottom edges. Remove from the oven and let cool for 10 to 15 minutes, or until just cool enough to handle. Keep the oven on.

7. Transfer the logs to a cutting board, and using a sharp chef's knife, cut the logs on an angle into generous ½-inch (13 mm) slices. (They will look a little undercooked in the middle.) Arrange the cookies, cut side down, back on the lined baking sheet. It will be a tight squeeze; it's not necessary to leave any space between the cookies. Return to the oven and bake for 6 to 8 minutes, until lightly golden on the underside. Remove the pan from the oven, carefully flip the biscotti over, and bake for 5 minutes more, until lightly golden all over. Let cool completely on the baking sheet. The cookies will keep in an airtight container at room temperature for up to 1 month.

Popovers
WITH SALTED MAPLE BUTTER

Popovers are traditionally made in popover pans—those funny-looking pans with deep, steep-sided individual cups welded to a wire rack—but you don't need one here. These popovers "pop up" beautifully in a standard muffin pan. The batter is somewhere between crepe batter and pancake batter, and creates popovers with a rich, custardy interior and crisp outer shell. In the oven, steam builds up inside the batter, pushing the popovers sky-high. It's pretty wild to watch through the oven window! Warm from the oven and slathered with maple butter, they taste like French toast in popover form.

Makes 12 popovers

FOR THE POPOVERS

3 tablespoons unsalted butter, melted and slightly cooled

5 large eggs

1 tablespoon sugar

1 teaspoon salt

1½ cups (360 mL) milk

1⅔ cups (217 g) all-purpose flour

Nonstick cooking spray with flour, such as Baker's Joy or Pam Baking

FOR THE MAPLE BUTTER

6 tablespoons (¾ stick/3 ounces/ 85 g) unsalted butter, at room temperature

3 tablespoons maple syrup, at room temperature

⅛ teaspoon salt

PRO TIP
Wondering why you put the muffin tin into the oven prior to filling it with batter? Pouring the batter into a hot pan maximizes the amount of steam generated, which equates to fluffier, lighter, taller popovers.

1. Preheat the oven to 375°F (190°C) and set an oven rack in the lower-middle position, allowing at least 5 inches of space above the rack for the popovers to rise. Place a 12-cup muffin pan in the oven while you make the batter.

2. Make the popovers: In a large mixing bowl, whisk together the melted butter, eggs, sugar, and salt. Whisk in half the milk. Add the flour and whisk until completely smooth. Add the remaining milk and whisk until combined.

3. Carefully remove the muffin pan from the oven and generously spray the whole pan, including the part between the cups, with nonstick cooking spray with flour. Pour or ladle the batter into the muffin cups, filling to just below the rim. Return the pan (remember it's hot!) to the oven and bake until golden brown, 40 to 50 minutes. Don't peek until after 35 minutes, or you'll risk the popovers deflating.

4. Make the maple butter: Combine the butter, maple syrup, and salt in the bowl of a handheld electric mixer fitted with the beaters. Beat until smooth and creamy, about 30 seconds. (Alternatively, use a fork to blend until smooth. It will take a minute or two for the mixture to come together.)

5. Lift the warm popovers out of the pan and onto a serving platter. Serve warm with the maple butter.

Panko-Crusted Salmon Cakes

When I told my friend and *Once Upon a Chef* right hand, Betsy Goldstein, about these salmon cakes, she said, "Hmmm . . . I think I'll wait until some of the reviews roll in to try those." I laughed because I knew she was thinking of the salmon cakes made from canned salmon that many of us grew up on. I promise: these are a whole different animal. Made from fresh raw salmon and seasoned with Old Bay, they're as elegant as crab cakes yet so much more affordable to make. What's more, they can be made entirely ahead of time and reheated. I love them for brunch over a green salad with a dollop of tartar sauce, but they also make a delicious dinner alongside Rice Pilaf (page 171) and Roasted Asparagus (page 173).

Serves 4 to 6 (makes 9 cakes)

¼ cup (60 g) best-quality mayonnaise, such as Hellmann's or Duke's

1 tablespoon fresh lemon juice (from 1 lemon)

1 teaspoon Dijon mustard

1 teaspoon Old Bay seasoning

¾ teaspoon salt

¼ teaspoon freshly ground black pepper

1¼ pounds (567 g) skinless salmon fillet, finely diced into ¼-inch (6 mm) pieces

1¼ cups (75 g) panko bread crumbs

¼ cup (12 g) scallions (dark and light green parts), thinly sliced (from 1 bunch)

⅓ cup (40 g) finely diced celery (from 2 stalks)

2 tablespoons finely chopped fresh dill

About ½ cup (120 mL) vegetable oil

Tartar Sauce (page 140) and lemon wedges, for serving

MAKE-AHEAD/FREEZER-FRIENDLY INSTRUCTIONS

The salmon cakes can be fully cooked and refrigerated up to 1 day ahead of time, or frozen for up to 3 months. To freeze, lay them out on a foil-lined baking sheet and cover loosely with plastic wrap. Freeze the patties in a single layer for about 1 hour, then remove them from the freezer and wrap the cakes individually in plastic. Freeze the wrapped cakes together in a resealable freezer bag or airtight container. Before serving, defrost them overnight in the refrigerator. To reheat: Preheat the oven to 350°F (175°C) and line a baking sheet with aluminum foil. Place the salmon cakes in the oven and cook until crisp on the exterior and warm throughout, 10 to 15 minutes.

SOURCING SAVVY

If buying a skin-on salmon fillet, purchase 1⅓ pounds (604 g) of fish to yield 1¼ (567 g) pounds of fish after skinning.

1. In a large bowl, whisk together the mayonnaise, lemon juice, mustard, Old Bay, salt, and pepper. Add the salmon, ¼ cup (15 g) of the panko, and the scallions, celery, and dill. Gently mix until uniform.

2. Place the remaining 1 cup (60 g) panko in a shallow dish or pie plate. Using a ⅓ (80 mL) measuring cup, scoop the salmon mixture and form it into a compact cake about 1 inch (2.5 cm) high. Place the salmon cake in the panko and gently coat it all over. Repeat with the remaining mixture to form about 9 cakes. (At this point, you can refrigerate the salmon cakes for up to 3 hours, until ready to cook, if you'd like.)

3. Pour the oil to a depth of ⅛ inch (3 mm) into a medium nonstick skillet. Heat over medium-high heat until shimmering. Place half the salmon cakes in the skillet and cook without moving until golden brown, about 2 minutes. Carefully flip the cakes and cook on the second side until golden brown, about 2 minutes more. Reduce the heat to medium if the cakes are browning too quickly. Transfer the cakes to a paper towel–lined plate to drain. Repeat with the remaining cakes (no need to change the oil). Serve warm.

Roasted Cherry Tomato & Basil Quiche

This quiche is a lovely brunch dish for a special occasion. Filled with burst cherry tomatoes and fresh basil, not only is it brimming with bright summer flavor, but it is also the prettiest quiche in my repertoire, hands down.

• PHOTOGRAPH ON PAGE 194

Serves 4 to 6

1 (9-inch/23 cm) deep-dish frozen pie crust shell (see Pro Tip)

1 pint (283 g) cherry tomatoes, halved

½ cup (60 g) thinly sliced shallot (from 1 large shallot)

2 tablespoons extra-virgin olive oil

1¼ teaspoons salt

4 large eggs

1¼ cups (300 mL) heavy cream

¼ teaspoon freshly ground black pepper

1 cup (4 ounces/120 g) finely shredded Gruyère cheese

¼ cup (25 g) finely grated Parmigiano-Reggiano cheese

3 tablespoons finely sliced fresh basil

1. Preheat the oven to 400°F (205°C) and set an oven rack in the middle position. Line a 13 x 18-inch (33 x 46 cm) baking sheet with heavy-duty aluminum foil. Remove the pie crust from the freezer and thaw until just soft enough to easily prick with a fork, about 10 minutes (if there are cracks in the crust; see Pro Tip, page 56).

2. Place the cherry tomatoes and shallot on the prepared baking sheet. Drizzle with the oil and sprinkle with ¾ teaspoon of the salt. Using a rubber spatula, toss to coat evenly. Roast until the tomatoes are shriveled and the shallot is softened, about 20 minutes, stirring once halfway through to promote even cooking. Holding onto the foil, lift the tomato mixture off the baking sheet and set aside on the counter to cool.

3. Place the pie crust on the baking sheet (the baking sheet will make it easy to move in and out of the oven). Prick the bottom and sides of the crust with a fork at 1-inch (2.5 cm) intervals. Bake until lightly golden, 10 to 15 minutes. Keep an eye on it; if it puffs up while cooking, gently prick it with a fork so that it will deflate. Set the crust aside and reduce the oven temperature to 325°F (165°C).

4. Meanwhile, in a medium bowl, whisk the eggs. Add the cream, pepper, and the remaining ½ teaspoon salt; whisk until evenly combined.

5. Arrange half the tomato mixture over the bottom of the crust. Top with the Gruyère, Parmigiano-Reggiano, and half the basil. Pour the egg mixture over the cheese, then scatter the remaining tomato mixture over it. Sprinkle the remaining basil over the top. Bake the quiche for 45 to 50 minutes, until the custard is set and lightly golden. Serve hot or warm.

MAKE-AHEAD/FREEZER-FRIENDLY INSTRUCTIONS

The quiche can be made up to 1 day ahead and refrigerated, or frozen for up to 3 months. After the quiche has cooled completely, wrap it securely with plastic wrap and then a layer of foil, making sure to fully seal all the edges. If frozen, thaw the quiche in the refrigerator overnight. Reheat, covered with foil, in a 325°F (165°C) oven for 35 to 45 minutes, or until hot in the center.

PRO TIP

If you'd like to use a homemade crust, follow the recipe on page 281. The only adjustment you'll need to make is in step 3. Instead of placing the slightly thawed and pricked store-bought crust in the oven, you'll need to take the homemade crust directly from the refrigerator, cover it with a piece of parchment paper (no need to prick it), and then fill it at least halfway full with dried beans or pie weights. Bake for about 15 minutes, or until the crust is pale and partially cooked. Remove the parchment paper and dried beans or pie weights and then proceed with the recipe.

"Lucky" Sausage & Cheddar Drop Biscuits

FREEZER-FRIENDLY INSTRUCTIONS

The biscuits can be fully prepared and frozen in a resealable freezer bag for up to 3 months. Reheat them directly from the freezer in a 300°F (150°C) oven for 15 to 20 minutes.

SOURCING SAVVY

I use the cooked frozen sausage links found near the waffles in the freezer section (which conveniently come in boxes with just the right amount).

PRO TIP

If you don't have buttermilk, you can easily make your own using milk and either white vinegar or fresh lemon juice. Add 1 tablespoon of vinegar or lemon juice to a liquid measuring cup and then add milk to the 1-cup (240 mL) line. Let the mixture sit for about 10 minutes. You'll begin to see small curdled bits; this means it's ready to add to the recipe.

My kids call these "lucky biscuits" because I make them on mornings when they have a big game or an important exam and I don't want them fueling up on sugary breakfast cereals. Filled with sausage and cheese, they taste like a gourmet version of a fast-food breakfast sandwich. Because of the sausage, the biscuits don't keep long, so freeze any you don't plan on eating right away; they reheat beautifully for breakfasts throughout the week.

Makes 10 biscuits

2 cups (260 g) all-purpose flour

3 tablespoons cornstarch

1 tablespoon baking powder

¼ teaspoon baking soda

1 teaspoon salt

1 tablespoon chopped fresh thyme, or 1 teaspoon dried

½ cup (1 stick/4 ounces/113 g) cold unsalted butter, cut into ½-inch (13 mm) chunks

1⅔ cups (7 ounces/198 g) thinly sliced cooked breakfast sausage links

1 cup (4 ounces/120 g) thickly shredded Cheddar cheese

1 cup (240 mL) buttermilk, plus a bit more as needed

1. Preheat the oven to 425°F (220°C) and set 2 racks in the centermost positions. Line two 13 x 18-inch (33 x 46 cm) baking sheets with parchment paper.

2. In the bowl of a food processor fitted with the metal blade, combine the flour, cornstarch, baking powder, baking soda, salt, and thyme; process for 10 seconds to blend. Add the butter and pulse until the mixture resembles coarse sand with pea-sized clumps of butter within. (Alternatively, you can mix the dry ingredients in a large bowl, then cut in the butter with a pastry cutter or rub it in with your fingers.)

3. Transfer the mixture to a large bowl. Stir in the sausage and cheese. Using a rubber spatula, fold in the buttermilk until the dough comes together in a craggy, sticky, evenly moistened mass. If the dough seems dry, add 1 to 2 tablespoons more buttermilk and mix again. Do not overmix.

4. Using 2 soup spoons, scoop 10 peach-size mounds (about 2½ inches/6 cm in diameter) of the biscuit dough onto the prepared baking sheets, spacing them evenly apart. Do not compact the mounds or try to smooth them on top; they are meant to have an irregular shape.

5. Bake the biscuits for 17 to 20 minutes, rotating the pans from top to bottom and front to back midway through, until the biscuits are golden brown. The biscuits are best served warm out of the oven. Once cool, freeze any biscuits you don't plan to serve right away.

Family Feasts

Seafood & Sausage Paella

SOURCING SAVVY

Smoked chorizo is usually located near the hot dogs and bacon in the supermarket. It is already fully cooked, and it is not necessary to remove the casings.

The recipe calls for Bomba or Spanish paella rice, a short-grain rice prized for its ability to absorb three times its volume in broth (rather than the normal two times) while still remaining firm, so it will never become sticky or mushy. You can find it in many grocery stores or order it online.

PRO TIP

A paella pan is useful and pretty if you have one, but there is no need to go out and buy one—you can use any large skillet to make paella.

Paella is a festive Spanish rice dish that takes its name from the wide, shallow pan in which it is traditionally cooked. It's one of our favorite dishes to share when we go out for Spanish food, and it's fun to make at home, too. I know it seems like a big to-do, and it can be if you add a wide variety of meats and seafood—the original paella from Valencia contains snails and rabbit—but I keep it relatively simple here by using only quick-cooking smoked chorizo, shrimp, and mussels. This is a feast!

Serves 6

5 tablespoons (75 mL) extra-virgin olive oil

12 ounces (340 g) smoked chorizo, sliced ½ inch (13 mm) thick on the bias (see Sourcing Savvy)

1 medium yellow onion, finely chopped

1 small red bell pepper, finely diced

3 large garlic cloves, finely chopped

1 tablespoon tomato paste

1½ cups (300 g) Bomba rice or other Spanish paella rice (see Sourcing Savvy)

3½ cups (840 mL) chicken broth

1 cup (240 mL) bottled clam juice

Generous pinch of saffron threads, about ⅛ teaspoon crumbled (see Sourcing Savvy, page 97)

1 bay leaf

Salt and freshly ground pepper

½ cup (60 g) frozen peas, thawed

1 tablespoon chopped fresh thyme

1 pound (454 g) large (31/35) shrimp, peeled and deveined

⅓ cup (80 mL) dry white wine

1 pound (454 g) mussels, scrubbed and debearded (see How to Store and Clean Mussels Prior to Cooking, page 98)

1. In a 13-inch (33 cm) paella pan (see Tip), a large enameled cast-iron pan (like a Le Creuset), or a large skillet, heat 2 tablespoons of the oil over medium heat. Cook the chorizo, flipping once, until lightly browned and some of the fat has rendered, about 3 minutes. Using a slotted spoon, transfer the chorizo to a plate. Add the onion and bell pepper to the pan and cook, stirring frequently, until softened, about 5 minutes. Add the garlic and cook 1 minute more. Stir in the tomato paste.

2. Add the rice and stir constantly, until coated with the vegetable mixture, about 2 minutes. Add the broth, clam juice, saffron, bay leaf, ¾ teaspoon salt, and ¼ teaspoon pepper; bring to a boil. Cover and simmer over low heat, without stirring, until the rice is cooked and most of the liquid is absorbed, about 15 minutes. Discard the bay leaf. Stir in the peas, then the chorizo (along with any accumulated juices) and the thyme; taste and adjust the seasoning if necessary. Remove the pan from the heat and cover.

3. In a separate large skillet, heat 2 tablespoons of the oil over medium heat until shimmering. Add the shrimp and sprinkle with ¼ teaspoon salt and a few

grinds of pepper; cook, turning once, until the shrimp are pink and cooked through, about 3 minutes. Add the shrimp to the paella and cover to keep warm.

4. In the same skillet that you cooked the shrimp (no need to rinse it first), bring the wine to a boil over medium heat. Add the mussels and cover with a lid; cook, shaking the skillet occasionally, until the mussels open, 2 to 4 minutes. Discard any mussels that have not opened. Pour the mussels and their cooking liquid over the paella.

5. Drizzle the remaining 1 tablespoon oil over the paella and serve.

Cioppino (Fisherman's Stew)

Brimming with fresh seafood in a tomato and wine broth that tastes like the sea, cioppino (pronounced cho-PEE-no) is a rustic Italian-American fish stew. Though the dish originated with Italian immigrant fishermen in San Francisco, my favorite version is served on the opposite coast at Portofino, a charming bayside restaurant in Longboat Key, Florida, where we celebrate my dad's birthday every year. One night, the chef was nice enough to share his recipe with me. To save time and simplify the recipe, I cut back on the variety of seafood called for (if you'd like to add more, crab, lobster, and mussels all make wonderful additions). Serve it with Garlic Toast (page 58), Focaccia with Tomatoes, Rosemary & Pecorino Romano (page 243), or a baguette for sopping up the broth—and don't forget a second bowl for shells and plenty of napkins.

Serves 4 to 6

6 tablespoons (90 mL) extra-virgin olive oil

⅔ cup (80 g) finely chopped shallot (from 2 medium shallots)

3 garlic cloves, minced

1 cup (240 mL) dry white wine

1 (28-ounce/794 g) can crushed tomatoes

2 cups (480 mL) bottled clam juice

2 teaspoons sugar

1¾ teaspoons salt

½ teaspoon red pepper flakes

½ teaspoon dried oregano

7 sprigs fresh thyme, plus 1 teaspoon chopped fresh thyme

1 cup (240 mL) water

1½ pounds (680 g) firm-fleshed fish fillets (such as halibut, cod, salmon, or red snapper), cut into 2-inch (5 cm) pieces

3 tablespoons unsalted butter

1½ pounds (680 g) littleneck clams, scrubbed (about 18) (see How to Buy and Prepare Clams for Cooking, page 224)

1½ pounds (680 g) extra-large (26/30) shrimp, peeled and deveined

Chopped fresh Italian parsley, for garnish (optional)

MAKE-AHEAD INSTRUCTIONS

The stew, without the seafood, can be made 2 days ahead and stored in the refrigerator. When ready to serve, bake the fish and bring the stew to a simmer before adding the seafood.

1. Preheat the oven to 400°F (205°C) and set an oven rack in the middle position. Line a 13 x 18-inch (33 x 46 cm) baking sheet with heavy-duty aluminum foil for easy cleanup.

2. In a large, heavy pot or Dutch oven, heat 4 tablespoons (60 mL) of the oil over medium heat. Add the shallot and cook, stirring frequently, until soft and translucent, about 5 minutes. Add the garlic and cook, stirring constantly, for 1 minute more. Do not brown.

-RECIPE CONTINUES-

3. Add the wine and increase the heat to high. Boil until the wine is reduced by about half, 3 to 4 minutes.

4. Add the crushed tomatoes, clam juice, sugar, 1 teaspoon of the salt, the red pepper flakes, oregano, thyme sprigs, and water. Bring to a boil, reduce the heat, and simmer, covered, for 25 minutes.

5. While the stew is simmering, toss the fish with the remaining 2 tablespoons oil and remaining ¾ teaspoon salt. Arrange the fish on the prepared baking sheet and bake for about 10 minutes, or until just cooked through. Cover and keep warm until ready to serve.

6. When the stew is done simmering, remove and discard the thyme sprigs and stir in the butter. Add the clams and bring the stew back to a simmer. Cover and cook for about 6 minutes, or until the clams have mostly opened. Gently stir in the shrimp and bring the stew back to a simmer; cover and cook until the shrimp are just cooked through and the clams are completely opened, about 5 minutes. Discard any unopened clams. Add the chopped thyme, then taste the stew and adjust the seasoning if necessary.

7. Divide the warm fish among serving bowls. Ladle the stew over top, dividing the clams and shrimp evenly among the bowls. Garnish with parsley, if using, and serve.

HOW TO BUY AND PREPARE CLAMS FOR COOKING

Littleneck clams are readily available at most supermarkets and are usually sold in a mesh bag because they are alive and need to breathe. If your fishmonger places them in a plastic bag, remove them from the bag immediately when you get home.

Check that the clams are alive by making sure all the shells are tightly closed. If any clams are open, gently tap them against the countertop; if they are alive, they will close their shells. Discard any clams that do not close their shells or that have cracked or chipped shells.

To clean, place all the clams in a bowl and cover them with cool tap water. Let the clams sit for 20 minutes to 1 hour. During this time, the clams will expel sand from inside their shells. When you're ready to cook, lift each clam from the water and rinse it, scrubbing if necessary, to get rid of any grit from the surface. (Note that most supermarkets sell farm-raised clams, which are already quite clean, so you may not find a lot of grit or sand.)

Crispy Buffalo Chicken Tenders

WITH BUFFALO SAUCE & RANCH DRESSING

Both of my parents hail from Buffalo, New York, so I was practically born with a love of food from Buffalo—Buffalo-style pizza, charcoal-broiled hot dogs, beef on weck, sponge candy, wings, and anything with Buffalo sauce—and I have passed that Buffalo food–loving gene on to my kids as well. This recipe is a spicy "Buffalo" version of the popular buttermilk fried chicken tenders from my website. It's perfect for Sunday night football, or any other time you're eating dinner in front of the TV. Kids love the tenders, especially dipped in homemade ranch dressing (don't tell my relatives, but blue cheese is a no-go in my house), and the extra kick from the hot sauce makes them a grown-up favorite, too. I keep it simple and serve the tenders and dips with carrot and celery sticks on the side.

Serves 6

FOR THE CHICKEN

2 pounds (907 g) chicken tenders, tendons trimmed

¾ cup plus 2 tablespoons (210 mL) buttermilk

2 tablespoons Frank's Red Hot Original hot sauce or similar brand

1½ teaspoons salt

¼ teaspoon garlic powder

½ teaspoon cayenne pepper

FOR THE BREADING

2¼ cups (293 g) all-purpose flour

2¼ teaspoons baking powder

1½ teaspoons salt

1 heaping teaspoon garlic powder

Heaping ¼ teaspoon cayenne pepper

4½ tablespoons (67 mL) buttermilk

FOR COOKING AND SERVING

3 to 4 cups (720 to 960 mL) vegetable or peanut oil, for frying

Buffalo Sauce (recipe follows), for dipping

Ranch dressing, homemade (recipe follows) or store-bought, for dipping

HEADS UP

Allow at least 3 hours to marinate the chicken.

MAKE-AHEAD INSTRUCTIONS

The ranch dressing can be made 2 days ahead and refrigerated.

FREEZER-FRIENDLY INSTRUCTIONS

The fried chicken tenders can be frozen for up to 3 months. To reheat, put the frozen tenders on a wire rack on top of a rimmed baking sheet and warm in a 350°F (175°C) oven until heated through and crisp, about 25 minutes, flipping halfway through.

PRO TIP

If you find that your chicken tenders have varying degrees of thickness, before adding them to the marinade, quickly even them out by applying a little pressure to the thicker areas with a flattened palm; this will ensure even cooking.

1. Marinate the chicken: In a resealable freezer bag, combine the chicken tenders with the buttermilk, hot sauce, salt, garlic powder, and cayenne. Seal the bag tightly and massage the chicken until it is evenly coated. Place the bag in a bowl (in case of leakage) and refrigerate for at least 3 hours or up to 24 hours.

2. Make the breading: In a large bowl, combine the flour, baking powder, salt, garlic powder, and cayenne. Whisk until well combined, then add the buttermilk and stir with a fork until the mixture is evenly clumpy.

3. Line a baking sheet with aluminum foil for easy cleanup. Remove the tenders from the marinade, a few at a time, and toss them in the flour mixture. Be sure to press the chicken firmly into the breading so clumps adhere to the

-RECIPE CONTINUES-

meat. (It's a messy job: use one hand to remove the wet tenders from the bag and the other to toss them in the breading.) Set the breaded chicken on the prepared baking sheet.

4. Fry the chicken: Line another baking sheet with a few layers of paper towels and set aside. Add the oil to a large Dutch oven or heavy-bottomed pot to reach a depth of about 1 inch (2.5 cm). Heat the oil over medium-high heat until it shimmers and registers 350°F/180°C on an instant-read thermometer (or test it by adding a small cube of fresh bread—if it sizzles immediately, the oil is hot enough). Using tongs, place several chicken tenders in the hot oil without crowding the pot. Cook until golden brown on the bottom side, 2 to 3 minutes, then flip and cook until the second side is also golden and the tenders are cooked through, 2 to 3 minutes more. Using tongs, set the cooked tenders on the paper towel–lined baking sheet to drain. Fry the remaining tenders in batches, adjusting the heat as necessary to maintain the frying temperature.

5. Serve the tenders with the Buffalo sauce and ranch dressing.

Buffalo Sauce   Makes about ¾ cup

6 tablespoons (90 mL) Frank's Red Hot Original hot sauce or a similar brand

6 tablespoons (¾ stick/3 ounces/ 85 g) unsalted butter, melted

In a small bowl, whisk together the hot sauce and melted butter. The sauce thickens as the butter cools; warm in the microwave, if necessary.

Ranch Dressing   Makes about 1⅓ cups

¾ cup (180 g) sour cream

¼ cup (60 mL) buttermilk or milk

¼ cup (60 g) best-quality mayonnaise, such as Hellmann's or Duke's

2 garlic cloves, minced

¾ teaspoon salt

¼ teaspoon freshly ground black pepper

⅛ teaspoon sugar

1½ teaspoons dried dill

¼ cup (10 g) finely chopped fresh chives

1 tablespoon fresh lemon juice (from 1 lemon)

Few dashes of Tabasco sauce (optional)

In a medium bowl, whisk together all the ingredients. Taste and adjust the seasoning if necessary. (The dressing is thick, like a dip. If you'd prefer it a little thinner, add a few more tablespoons of buttermilk or milk to thin it out.)

Coq au Vin

Rich and brimming with flavor, coq au vin is a classic French stew of chicken braised in red wine, with mushrooms and crispy lardons made from bacon or pancetta. It's the perfect cooking project to tackle on a chilly weekend when you've got a few hours to burn. I learned to make it in culinary school using a cut-up whole chicken (a *coq* is an old rooster), but I prefer to use bone-in chicken thighs only. The thighs remain tender and succulent when braised for a long time, whereas white meat tends to dry out. My recipe omits the traditional garnish of pearl onions, as they can be difficult to find, and I actually prefer the stew without them.

As with most stews, this is even better the next day and freezes well, too. Serve it with Rice Pilaf (page 171), buttered egg noodles, mashed potatoes, or crusty bread—basically anything to soak up the gorgeously full-flavored sauce.

Serves 6

3 tablespoons olive oil

4 ounces (114 g) diced pancetta or bacon

8 bone-in, skin-on chicken thighs (about 4 pounds/1.8 kg), trimmed of excess fat and skin

Salt and freshly ground black pepper

1 large yellow onion, roughly chopped

4 garlic cloves, roughly chopped

¼ cup (60 mL) cognac

2½ cups (600 mL) dry red wine, preferably Burgundy/Pinot Noir

2½ cups (600 mL) chicken broth

1½ tablespoons tomato paste

2 teaspoons balsamic vinegar

1½ teaspoons sugar

1 tablespoon fresh thyme leaves, or 1 teaspoon dried

1 bay leaf

3 large carrots, peeled and cut into ½-inch (13 mm) chunks on the bias

8 ounces (227 g) cremini mushrooms, sliced

4 tablespoons (½ stick/2 ounces/ 57 g) unsalted butter, softened

4 tablespoons (33 g) all-purpose flour

MAKE-AHEAD/FREEZER-FRIENDLY INSTRUCTIONS

The stew can be made up to 2 days ahead and refrigerated. (For best results, store the mushrooms and pancetta in separate containers in the refrigerator and add before serving.) Leftovers can be frozen in an airtight container for up to 3 months. If frozen, defrost in the refrigerator overnight and then reheat it on the stovetop over medium heat.

SOURCING SAVVY

Pancetta is simply Italian bacon. Instead of being smoked like American bacon, it is cured with salt and spices and then dried. You can find it at the deli at most supermarkets or pre-cut and packaged in the refrigerated gourmet foods aisle, which is a great time-saver.

PRO TIP

I cook the thighs with the skin on to render the fat and lend flavor, but I remove it before serving; it gets soggy and the dish is more appetizing without it.

1. Heat 1 tablespoon of the oil in a large (5-quart/5 L) Dutch oven or heavy-bottomed pot over medium heat. Add the pancetta and cook until the fat has rendered and the pancetta is crispy, 5 to 8 minutes. Using a slotted spoon, transfer the pancetta to a paper towel–lined plate, leaving the fat in the pan.

2. Season the chicken all over with 2 teaspoons salt and ½ teaspoon pepper. Increase the heat to medium-high and brown half the chicken in a single layer, skin side down, until golden and crispy, about 5 minutes (brown on the skin side only). Using tongs, transfer the chicken to a plate; set aside. Repeat with the remaining chicken. Pour off all but about 2 tablespoons of the fat.

-RECIPE CONTINUES-

3. Return the pot to the stove and reduce the heat to medium low. Add the onion and cook, stirring occasionally, until softened and just starting to brown, 3 to 5 minutes. Add the garlic and cook, stirring constantly, until fragrant, about 1 minute more. Add the cognac and cook, stirring to scrape the browned bits from the bottom of the pan, until the cognac has evaporated. Add the wine, broth, tomato paste, vinegar, sugar, thyme, bay leaf, and ½ teaspoon salt. Bring to a boil, then reduce the heat to medium and boil gently, uncovered, for 15 minutes.

4. Add the chicken, along with any accumulated juices, to the pot; add the carrots. Bring to a simmer, then cover and cook over low heat for 30 minutes, until the chicken and carrots are cooked through.

5. While the chicken cooks, heat the remaining 2 tablespoons oil in a large skillet over medium heat. Add the mushrooms and ¼ teaspoon salt and cook, stirring frequently, until the mushrooms are golden brown, about 5 minutes.

6. In a small bowl, mash the softened butter and flour to make a smooth paste.

7. Using a slotted spoon, transfer the cooked chicken to a plate. Increase the heat under the pot to medium and stir in three-fourths of the flour and butter paste. Gently boil until the sauce is thickened, 5 to 7 minutes; add the remaining paste if you'd like the sauce a little thicker. Fish out and discard the bay leaf.

8. Using a fork and knife, pull the skin off of the chicken and discard.

9. Add the chicken and any accumulated juices to the pot and simmer, uncovered, for about 10 minutes. Right before serving, stir in the browned mushrooms and pancetta. Taste and adjust the seasoning if necessary, and serve.

Latin-Style Roast Pork

WITH LIME CHIMICHURRI SAUCE

Inspired by the succulent, highly seasoned pork dishes made throughout Latin America—from Puerto Rican *pernil,* to Cuban mojo-marinated pork shoulder, to Mexican carnitas—this is one of my favorite things to cook when I've got a full house. The pork is rubbed with a mixture of aromatics, herbs, and spices, and then it is cooked low and slow over a bed of onions until juicy and fall-apart tender. It makes the house smell amazing, feeds a crowd inexpensively, and makes fabulous leftovers for quesadillas, tacos, and sandwiches. Chimichurri sauce is a zesty, bright green condiment from Argentina that is delicious on grilled or roasted meats; it complements and brightens the rich flavor of the pork.

Serve with corn tortillas or rice and Black Beans with Onions, Garlic & Spices (page 235).

Serves 8 to 10

FOR THE ROAST PORK

1 (5- to 6-pound/2.3 to 2.7 kg) bone-in pork butt (Boston butt), fat cap trimmed to about ⅛ inch (3 mm) thick

2 large yellow onions, halved and sliced ¼ inch (6 mm) thick

2 teaspoons paprika

2 teaspoons ground cumin

1 tablespoon salt

¾ teaspoon freshly ground black pepper

5 garlic cloves

½ cup (60 g) roughly chopped shallot (from 1 large shallot)

½ cup (16 g) packed cilantro leaves and tender stems (from 1 bunch)

3 tablespoons extra-virgin olive oil

2 cups (480 mL) water

FOR THE CHIMICHURRI SAUCE

¾ cup (180 mL) extra-virgin olive oil

6 tablespoons (90 mL) fresh lime juice (from 3 limes)

3 garlic cloves, roughly chopped

⅔ cup (80 g) roughly chopped shallot (from 2 medium shallots)

1 teaspoon salt

½ teaspoon red pepper flakes

3 cups (96 g) packed cilantro leaves and tender stems (from 1 to 2 bunches)

1. Make the roast pork: Preheat the oven to 275°F (135°C) and set an oven rack in the lower-middle position. Pat the pork dry with paper towels.

2. Arrange the sliced onions in a single layer in the bottom of a small (12 x 14-inch/ 30 x 36 cm) roasting pan.

-RECIPE CONTINUES-

3. In a food processor, combine the paprika, cumin, salt, pepper, garlic, shallot, cilantro, and oil. Process, scraping down the sides of the bowl as necessary, until the mixture is smooth, thick, and rust-colored.

4. Set the pork butt on a work surface with the fat side down. Using a rubber spatula, smear some of the wet rub over the top of the roast. Flip the roast over and place it, fat side up, on top of the onions in the roasting pan. Smear the remaining wet rub over the top and sides of the pork, so the whole roast is covered.

5. Pour the water around the pork. Roast, uncovered, until the meat is fork-tender and a thermometer inserted into the thickest part registers 200°F (93°C), 6 to 7 hours.

6. Remove the pork from the oven and tent it with aluminum foil; let it rest for about 10 minutes.

7. Make the chimichurri sauce: Meanwhile, in a food processor, combine the oil, lime juice, garlic, shallots, salt, red pepper flakes, and cilantro; process until finely chopped.

8. Finish the pork: Transfer the roast to a cutting board. Using a slotted spoon, remove the onions from the pan juices and place them in a small bowl. Pour the pan juices into another small bowl and let sit for a few minutes until the fat begins to separate from the juices. Spoon off the fat and discard it. Pour the skimmed juices back into the pan. Place the onions back into the roasting pan as well.

9. While the pork is still warm, use 2 forks to pull the meat into large irregular chunks, removing and discarding any large pieces of fat or sinew. Transfer the meat to the roasting pan and toss it with the pan juices and onions. Spoon the meat onto a serving platter and serve immediately with the chimichurri sauce on the side.

Black Beans

WITH ONIONS, GARLIC & SPICES

A little soupy and a lot flavorful, these quick and easy Cuban-inspired black beans make a delicious side dish to my Latin-Style Roast Pork (page 231). You can also serve them over rice for a satisfying meatless meal (to make them vegetarian, replace the chicken broth with vegetable broth). I usually provide specific salt measurements, but since different brands of beans and chicken broth have different sodium levels, it's best to season to taste.

PRO TIP

If you'd like to reduce the recipe, you'll also need to reduce the simmering time; just cook until the beans are thickened to your liking.

Serves 8

¼ cup (60 mL) extra-virgin olive oil

1 medium red onion, finely chopped

5 garlic cloves, minced

3 (15.5-ounce/439 g) cans black beans, drained and rinsed

1¼ cups (300 mL) chicken broth

1 teaspoon ground cumin

1 teaspoon dried oregano

¼ teaspoon ground coriander

Salt

1. In a large Dutch oven or heavy pot, heat the oil over medium heat. Add the onion and cook, stirring occasionally, until softened and translucent, about 4 minutes. Add the garlic and cook, stirring frequently, for 2 minutes more. Do not brown.

2. Add about one-third of the beans to the pot; using a potato masher or the back of a fork, coarsely mash the beans until they are broken up. Add the remaining beans, the broth, cumin, oregano, and coriander. Bring to a gentle boil, then reduce the heat to low and simmer, uncovered, stirring occasionally, for 5 to 6 minutes, or until thickened to your liking. Add salt to taste and serve.

Chicken Chili & Cornbread Pie

MAKE-AHEAD INSTRUCTIONS

The chicken chili can be made up to 2 days ahead. Reheat it in the microwave or on the stovetop before adding the cornbread topping and baking.

SOURCING SAVVY

When purchasing ground chicken for this recipe, be sure avoid any packages marked "extra lean."

PRO TIP

If you have a food processor, this recipe is a good reason to break it out. It makes quick work of chopping the veggies (and it also chops them very fine, so you can conceal them from your kids, if need be—just be careful not to puree them).

This comforting Tex-Mex casserole combines two of my kids' favorite foods in one big dish: chili and cornbread. Loaded with veggies, beans, and lots of cheese, it is a hearty crowd-pleaser for all ages. I use a 13-inch cast iron skillet to make the recipe in one pan that can go from stovetop to oven—feel free to do the same—but since most people don't have a cast iron skillet that large, the instructions call for making the chili in a sauté pan and then transferring it to a baking dish before topping it with the cornbread batter.

Serves 6 to 8

FOR THE CHICKEN CHILI

3 tablespoons vegetable oil

1 medium yellow onion, finely chopped

1 green bell pepper, finely chopped

1 red bell pepper, finely chopped

4 garlic cloves, finely chopped

2 pounds (907 g) ground chicken (see Sourcing Savvy)

1 teaspoon smoked paprika

1 tablespoon ancho chile powder

1 tablespoon ground cumin

1 teaspoon dried oregano

1/8 to 1/4 teaspoon cayenne pepper (optional)

1¾ teaspoons salt

1 (15-ounce/425 g) can tomato sauce

1 (15.5-ounce/439 g) can black beans, drained and rinsed

2 cups (240 g) shredded pepper Jack cheese

¼ cup (10 g) chopped fresh cilantro

Nonstick cooking spray

FOR THE CORNBREAD TOPPING

¾ cup (98 g) all-purpose flour

¾ cup (105 g) fine yellow cornmeal

1½ tablespoons sugar

2 teaspoons baking powder

½ teaspoon salt

1 cup (240 mL) milk

1 large egg

4 tablespoons (½ stick/2 ounces/ 56 g) unsalted butter, melted

1. Make the chicken chili: Heat the oil in a large sauté pan over medium heat. Add the onion, bell peppers, and garlic and cook, stirring occasionally, until soft and just starting to brown, 10 to 15 minutes. Add the chicken, paprika, chile powder, cumin, oregano, cayenne (if using), and salt. Increase the heat to high; use a wooden spoon to stir and break the chicken into small clumps. Cook, stirring frequently, until the chicken is partially cooked, about

-RECIPE CONTINUES-

5 minutes. Stir in the tomato sauce, then reduce the heat to medium low. Simmer, stirring occasionally to break the chicken into smaller clumps, until the chicken is cooked through, about 5 minutes. Stir in the beans, cheese, and cilantro. Taste and the adjust seasoning if necessary.

2. Lightly grease a 9 x 13-inch (23 x 33 cm) baking dish with nonstick cooking spray or butter. Carefully transfer the chicken mixture to the baking dish and pat it into an even layer. Let it sit while you make the topping.

3. Preheat the oven to 400°F (205°C) and set an oven rack in the middle position.

4. Make the cornbread topping: In a medium bowl, whisk together the flour, cornmeal, sugar, baking powder, and salt. In a small bowl, whisk together the milk and egg. Make a well in the center of the dry ingredients; add the milk/egg mixture and the melted butter. Whisk until uniform and no lumps remain.

5. Pour the cornbread batter evenly over the chicken mixture. It will seem like a thin layer; that's okay, it will puff up in the oven. Transfer the baking dish to the oven and bake until the cornbread is golden and the chicken mixture is bubbling, 25 to 35 minutes. Transfer to a wire rack and cool for at least 10 minutes before serving.

Italian Wedding Soup

My kids love anything with meatballs in it (especially mini meatballs), so there's always excitement at our house when this soup is on the menu. The name "wedding soup" comes from the Italian phrase *minestra maritata*—or "married soup"—which is a reference to the way the flavors combine, like a happy marriage. The challenge in preparing a delicious wedding soup is that the broth is traditionally made from a rich, long-cooked homemade chicken stock. I have to admit I don't make my own stock, even on the weekends. To mimic the rich flavor, I use high-quality store-bought broth (see Sourcing Savvy) fortified with wine and lots of vegetables. For the meatballs, my secret is to add ground sausage to the beef mixture, which adds tons of flavor without the need for lots of other seasonings. The most tedious part of the recipe is rolling the little meatballs—the recipe makes 50!—but I usually get one of the kids to help.

Serves 6 to 8

FOR THE MEATBALLS

Nonstick cooking spray

1 large egg

3 tablespoons finely chopped fresh chives

2 teaspoons finely chopped fresh sage

2 garlic cloves, minced

¾ pound (340 g) 85% or 90% lean ground beef

½ pound (227 g) sweet or hot Italian sausage, removed from the casings

½ cup (50 g) finely grated Parmigiano-Reggiano cheese

⅓ cup (47 g) seasoned Italian bread crumbs

¼ teaspoon salt

FOR THE SOUP

2 tablespoons olive oil

1 medium yellow onion, diced

2 large carrots, diced

2 celery stalks, diced

6 cups (1.4 L) best-quality chicken broth

2 cups (480 mL) best-quality beef broth

2 cups (480 mL) water

½ cup (120 mL) dry white wine

1 bay leaf

½ teaspoon salt

¼ teaspoon white pepper

1 cup (150 g) small pasta, such as ditalini

3 cups (100 g) packed stemmed and chopped fresh spinach

Finely grated Parmigiano-Reggiano cheese, for serving

-RECIPE CONTINUES-

FREEZER-FRIENDLY INSTRUCTIONS

The soup can be frozen for up to 3 months, but wait until you reheat the soup to add the pasta. Defrost the soup in the refrigerator for 12 hours and then reheat it on the stovetop over medium heat until gently boiling. Add the pasta and cook until tender.

SOURCING SAVVY

For best results, I recommend using Swanson brand chicken and beef broths. Avoid low-sodium broth as it makes the soup taste bland.

1. Make the meatballs: Preheat the oven to 350°F (175°C) and set an oven rack in the middle position. Line a baking sheet with aluminum foil and set a wire rack on top. Spray the rack generously with nonstick cooking spray.

2. In a large bowl, beat the egg with the chives, sage, and garlic. Add the ground beef, sausage, Parmigiano-Reggiano, bread crumbs, and salt and mix with your hands until evenly combined. Roll the mixture into tablespoon-sized balls (about 1 inch/2.5 cm in diameter) and place on the prepared rack. Bake for 15 to 18 minutes, until lightly browned and cooked through.

3. Make the soup: Meanwhile, heat the oil in a large Dutch oven or heavy pot over medium heat. Add the onion, carrots, and celery and cook, stirring frequently, until the vegetables are softened, about 8 minutes. Add the chicken broth, beef broth, water, wine, bay leaf, salt, and pepper and bring to a boil. Add the pasta and cook, uncovered, at a gentle boil until the pasta is al dente, 8 to 10 minutes (or according to the package directions). Taste the soup and adjust the seasoning if necessary.

4. Reduce the heat to low and add the spinach and meatballs to the pot. Simmer for a few minutes, until the spinach is wilted and the meatballs are warmed through. Ladle the soup into bowls and serve with grated Parmigiano-Reggiano.

Focaccia

WITH TOMATOES, ROSEMARY & PECORINO ROMANO

Perfect for a hungry crowd, focaccia is a rich and flavorful Italian flatbread baked in a sheet pan. It is one of the easiest, most forgiving yeast breads to make, and it's a fun weekend baking project to tackle with kids, too. To give the bread its signature dimpled appearance, you use your fingers to form small indentations all over the dough. These "dimples" hold little pools of olive oil that soak into the bread as it bakes. The recipe calls for about 1 cup of oil, which I know seems like a lot, but that's what makes focaccia so good! Note that the oil is added in stages, so be sure to read the recipe carefully before starting lest you accidentally add it all at once. Serve as a tasty snack, appetizer, or table bread.

Serves 10 to 12 (about 24 pieces)

5 cups (650 g) all-purpose flour, plus more for kneading

1 tablespoon sugar

2¼ teaspoons (1 packet) instant/rapid-rise yeast

1 tablespoon plus 1 teaspoon kosher salt

1¾ cups (420 mL) warm water

About 1 cup (240 mL) extra-virgin olive oil

1 pound (454 g) vine-ripened tomatoes, sliced ⅛ inch (3 mm) thick

2 garlic cloves, minced

1 heaping tablespoon chopped fresh rosemary (from several sprigs)

¼ cup (25 g) finely grated pecorino Romano cheese

MAKE-AHEAD/FREEZER-FRIENDLY INSTRUCTIONS

Focaccia is best eaten freshly baked, but it can be made up to 1 day ahead of time. Wrap the focaccia in aluminum foil and place it in a resealable freezer bag at room temperature. Reheat, wrapped in foil, in a 350°F (175°C) oven until warmed through, 10 to 15 minutes. The focaccia can also be cut into portions, wrapped in plastic wrap and then foil, and frozen for up to 3 months.

PRO TIP

If your oven has a proof setting, that's the ideal spot to let the dough rise. A sunny spot in the kitchen is also a good option.

1. In the bowl of a stand mixer fitted with the dough hook, combine the flour, sugar, yeast, and 1 tablespoon of the salt. Mix on low speed to combine. Add the water and ½ cup (120 mL) of the oil; mix on low speed until the dough comes together. Turn up the speed to medium low and continue to knead for 5 to 6 minutes, until the dough becomes soft and slightly tacky. It should stick to the bottom of the bowl a bit. If the dough seems too wet, sprinkle it with a few tablespoons of flour and turn the mixer back on to knead it briefly to combine.

2. Transfer the dough to a clean, lightly floured work surface (it helps to flour your hands, too). Knead briefly until the dough comes together into a smooth ball. Coat the inside of a large bowl with about 1 teaspoon of the oil. Place the dough in the bowl, flipping it once so that both the top and bottom are lightly slicked with oil. Cover the bowl with plastic wrap and set it aside in a warm, draft-free spot until the dough has doubled in size, 1 to 2 hours.

-RECIPE CONTINUES-

3. Coat a 13 x 18-inch (33 x 46 cm) rimmed baking sheet with ¼ cup (60 mL) of the oil. Plop the dough onto the baking sheet and begin pressing it out with your hands to fit the size of the pan. Turn the dough over once to coat both sides with oil. Continue to stretch the dough to fit the pan. Once the dough is stretched, spread your fingers out and make impressions almost all the way through the dough (don't poke holes; just press down to the bottom of the pan). Cover the baking sheet with plastic wrap and place it in a warm, draft-free spot until the dough has puffed up and doubled in size, about 1 hour.

4. While the dough is rising a second time, preheat the oven to 425°F (220°C) and set an oven rack in the middle position. Place a few layers of paper towels on a large cutting board. Arrange the sliced tomatoes on the paper towels and cover them with a few more layers of paper towels. Press gently to extract some of the liquid from the tomatoes. (This step prevents the focaccia from getting soggy.) Let the tomatoes sit, covered with paper towels, until ready to use.

5. When the dough is ready, arrange the tomatoes on top of the dough, spaced evenly; do not overlap. Combine the garlic with the remaining 3 tablespoons oil. Spoon the oil and garlic mixture over the tomato slices. Sprinkle the remaining teaspoon of kosher salt, the rosemary, and the cheese over the top.

6. Bake until lightly golden on top and crispy on the bottom, about 25 minutes. Remove the focaccia from the oven and let it cool in the pan on a wire rack for about 15 minutes. Transfer the focaccia to a cutting board and slice into squares.

Five-Star Beef Stew
WITH CARROTS & POTATOES

With more than 3,000 five-star reviews, this classic French beef stew is the all-time most popular recipe on my website. It is the ultimate winter comfort food. Chunks of well-marbled beef are seared in a hot pan, then gently braised with garlic and onions in a rich wine-based broth. After a few hours in the oven, the meat becomes meltingly tender and enveloped in a deeply flavorful sauce. It takes a few hours to make, but the recipe is mostly hands-off. Go ahead and make it a day or two ahead of time; the flavor improves the longer it sits.

Serves 6

3 pounds (1.4 kg) boneless beef chuck, cut into 1½-inch (4 cm) pieces (see Sourcing Savvy)

2 teaspoons salt

1 teaspoon freshly ground black pepper

3 tablespoons olive oil

2 medium yellow onions, cut into 1-inch (2.5 cm) chunks

7 garlic cloves, peeled and smashed

2 tablespoons balsamic vinegar

1½ tablespoons tomato paste

¼ cup (33 g) all-purpose flour

2 cups (480 mL) dry red wine

2 cups (480 mL) beef broth

2 cups (480 mL) water

1 bay leaf

½ teaspoon dried thyme

1½ teaspoons sugar

4 large carrots, peeled and cut into 1-inch (2.5 cm) chunks on an angle

1 pound (454 g) small white boiling potatoes (baby Yukon Golds), cut in half

Chopped fresh Italian parsley, for serving (optional)

MAKE-AHEAD/FREEZER-FRIENDLY INSTRUCTIONS

The stew can be made up to 2 days ahead and refrigerated, or frozen for up to 3 months. If freezing, do not add the potatoes; they become soft and grainy when frozen. If you'd like, boil some potatoes separately when you defrost the stew and either add them into the stew or serve them on the side. If frozen, defrost the stew in the refrigerator overnight and then reheat on the stovetop over medium heat.

SOURCING SAVVY

Look for chuck roast that is well-marbled, meaning it should have a good number of white veins of fat running through it. Avoid meat generically packaged as "stew meat," especially if it looks lean.

1. Preheat the oven to 325°F (165°C) and set an oven rack in the lower-middle position.

2. Pat the beef dry and season it with the salt and pepper. In a large Dutch oven or heavy soup pot, heat 1 tablespoon of the oil over medium-high heat until hot and shimmering. Brown the meat in 3 batches, turning it with tongs, about 5 minutes per batch; add another tablespoon of oil for the other 2 batches. (To sear the meat properly, do not crowd the pan, and make sure you let the meat develop a nice brown crust before turning with tongs.) Transfer the meat to a large plate and set aside.

3. Add the onions, garlic, and vinegar; cook, stirring with a wooden spoon and scraping the browned bits from the bottom of the pan, for about 5 minutes. Add the tomato paste and cook for 1 minute more. Add the beef with its juices to the pan and sprinkle with the flour. Cook, stirring with a wooden spoon,

-RECIPE CONTINUES-

until the flour is dissolved, 1 to 2 minutes. Add the wine, broth, water, bay leaf, thyme, and sugar. Stir with a wooden spoon to loosen any additional browned bits from the bottom of the pan and bring to a boil. Cover the pot with a lid, transfer to the oven, and braise for 2 hours.

4. Remove the pot from the oven and add the carrots and potatoes. Cover and place back in the oven for about 1 hour more, or until the vegetables are cooked, the broth is thickened, and the meat is tender. Fish out and discard the bay leaf, then taste and adjust the seasoning if necessary. Sprinkle with the parsley, if using, and serve. (Alternatively, let the stew cool to room temperature, and store it in the refrigerator overnight. When ready to serve, reheat the stew on the stovetop over medium heat until warmed through, then sprinkle it with fresh parsley, if using, and serve.)

Sear-Roasted Beef Tenderloin
WITH HORSERADISH CREAM SAUCE

PRO TIPS

Butchers often tie tenderloins near the tapered ends to give them an even thickness. If your tenderloin comes tied that way, leave the string on until after it's cooked.

—

I know it can be nerve-wracking to cook an expensive cut like beef tenderloin, but if you have a meat thermometer with a remote probe, the process is completely stress-free. You can monitor the temperature of the meat as it cooks, and you'll know it's perfectly done without ever opening your oven door—no poking, cutting, peeking, or guesswork involved.

When I was working at Sam & Harry's, a fine-dining steakhouse in Washington, D.C., which was an "it" spot for D.C.'s movers and shakers in the 1990s, we served sliced beef tenderloin with horseradish sauce for almost all our private cocktail parties. It's just as good at room temperature as it is hot, so it's ideal for a buffet—and if you're serving finger food, you can offer brioche slider buns so your guests can make mini steak sandwiches. Who wouldn't love that?

Serves 4 to 8

FOR THE ROAST

1 (2- to 4-pound/907 g to 1.8 kg) center-cut beef tenderloin roast

Kosher salt (½ teaspoon per pound of beef)

Freshly ground black pepper (¼ teaspoon per pound of beef)

2 tablespoons vegetable oil

FOR THE HORSERADISH SAUCE

¾ cup (180 g) sour cream

¾ cup (180 g) best-quality mayonnaise, such as Hellmann's or Duke's

2 tablespoons prepared horseradish

2 tablespoons Dijon mustard

½ teaspoon kosher salt

¼ teaspoon freshly ground black pepper

2 tablespoons finely chopped fresh chives

1. Make the roast: Let the beef stand at room temperature for 1 hour before roasting. Preheat the oven to 400°F (205°C) and set an oven rack in the middle position.

2. Pat the beef dry with a paper towel and season all over with salt and pepper. Heat the oil in a large ovenproof skillet over medium-high heat until almost smoking. Sear the beef, turning it with tongs, until well browned on all but one side (leave one of the wider sides unseared), 8 to 10 minutes total. Turn the tenderloin unseared side down and transfer the skillet to the oven. (If your skillet isn't ovenproof, transfer the beef to a lightly oiled roasting pan.)

3. Roast until a meat thermometer inserted into the center of the tenderloin registers about 125°F (52°C) for medium-rare, 15 to 25 minutes, or until done to your liking (120°F/49°C for rare, 130°F/54°C for medium). Keep in mind that the roast's internal temperature will continue to rise several degrees as it rests. When you take the roast out of the oven, place a dish towel or oven mitt over the skillet handle to remind yourself that it's hot (trust me, it's easy to forget and burn yourself!).

4. Transfer the roast to a carving board (preferably with a well for collecting juices) and let it rest, covered loosely with aluminum foil, for 10 to 15 minutes (or up to 1 hour if serving at room temperature).

5. Make the horseradish sauce: Meanwhile, in a small bowl, whisk the sour cream, mayonnaise, horseradish, mustard, salt, pepper, and chives until combined. Taste and adjust the seasoning if necessary.

6. Carve the tenderloin into ½-inch-thick (13 mm) slices. Serve the beef warm or at room temperature, with the horseradish sauce on the side.

Decadent Desserts

Strawberries & Cream Layer Cake

Strawberry season coincides with my husband's June birthday. Since he is a huge strawberry shortcake lover, I created this lemon-kissed strawberry "shortcake" layer cake for him. Topped with a few tall sparklers, it makes a stunning birthday cake. This cake will be only as good as the berries you put in it, so be sure the fruit is nice and sweet. I like to leave the stems on a few of the strawberries and use them for decorating the top of the cake.

Serves 10 to 12

FOR THE CAKE

Nonstick cooking spray with flour, such as Baker's Joy or Pam Baking

2 cups (260 g) all-purpose flour

3 tablespoons cornstarch

½ teaspoon baking soda

Heaping ¼ teaspoon salt

¾ cup (180 mL) buttermilk

1 tablespoon grated lemon zest

2 tablespoons fresh lemon juice (from 1 lemon)

¾ cup (1½ sticks/6 ounces/170 g) unsalted butter, at room temperature

1¾ cups (350 g) granulated sugar

3 large eggs

FOR THE FILLING

6 ounces (170 g) cream cheese, at room temperature

1½ cups (174 g) confectioners' sugar

1 tablespoon fresh lemon juice (from 1 lemon)

Pinch of salt

1¾ cups (420 mL) heavy cream, cold

1½ pounds (680 g) fresh strawberries, hulled and sliced about ½ inch (13 mm) thick

1. Make the cake: Preheat the oven to 350°F (175°C) and set an oven rack in the middle position. Spray two 9-inch (23 cm) cake pans with nonstick cooking spray with flour.

2. In a medium bowl, whisk together the flour, cornstarch, baking soda, and salt.

3. In a small bowl, whisk together the buttermilk, lemon zest, and lemon juice.

4. In the bowl of an electric mixer fitted with the paddle attachment or beaters, cream the butter and sugar on medium speed until light and fluffy, 3 to 4 minutes. Scrape down the sides of the bowl, then beat in the eggs

-RECIPE CONTINUES-

one at a time, beating well after each addition. Scrape down the sides of the bowl again. With the mixer on low speed, beat in one-fourth of the flour mixture, then one-third of the buttermilk mixture. Beat in another fourth of the flour, then another third of the buttermilk mixture. Repeat with another fourth of the flour and the remaining buttermilk mixture. Finally, beat in the remaining flour mixture. Scrape down the sides of the bowl and give a quick mix to make sure all the ingredients are well incorporated.

5. Divide the batter between the prepared pans and spread with an offset spatula. (Note that the batter will only come about ½ inch [13 mm] up the sides of the pan; don't worry—it rises quite a bit.) Bake for 20 to 22 minutes, until the cakes are lightly golden and a tester comes out clean. Set the cakes on a cooling rack and let cool for 15 minutes. Invert the cakes onto the rack to cool completely.

6. Make the filling: In the bowl of an electric mixer fitted with the paddle attachment or beaters, beat the cream cheese, confectioners' sugar, lemon juice, and salt on medium-low speed until smooth and creamy, scraping down the sides of the bowl as necessary. (If using a stand mixer, now switch the paddle attachment to the whisk.) With the mixer on low speed, slowly pour in the cream and mix until incorporated. Increase the speed to medium and beat until stiff peaks form, a few minutes.

7. Place one cake layer on a cake platter or pedestal. Arrange about half the strawberries, cut side down, on top of the cake, covering as much of the surface as possible. (For this layer, try to use strawberries of about the same size so they create a level base for the top layer of the cake.) Dollop half the cream filling over the strawberries and spread evenly to the edges to cover the berries. Place the second cake layer on top. Dollop the remaining cream filling over the top cake layer; using an offset spatula, spread the cream filling to the edges in a pretty swirl pattern. Decorate the top with the remaining strawberries. Use a sharp knife to slice the cake. Store any leftover cake, covered, in the refrigerator for up to 3 days; bring to room temperature before serving.

Butterscotch Pudding
WITH SALTED CARAMEL SAUCE

This is my take on the famous butterscotch budino from Pizzeria Mozza in Los Angeles. It is nostalgic yet sophisticated, and one spoonful will make grown men close their eyes and sigh with delight. It is a true butterscotch pudding, meaning it is made by first cooking brown sugar until it is deeply caramelized. Many butterscotch pudding recipes skip this important step—the word *butterscotch* is thrown around loosely, and it is often used to describe confections made simply with butter and brown sugar—but browning the sugar is the key to depth of flavor. If you skip it, your pudding may look like butterscotch, but it will taste like vanilla.

   Though the recipe looks long, it's not difficult. That said, you'll need to stand near the stove with a timer and watch the caramelization process carefully. The microwave caramel sauce is modestly adapted from *Cook's Illustrated*; it's incredible, and you won't believe how easy it is to make.

Serves 6

FOR THE PUDDING

4 large egg yolks

¼ cup (35 g) cornstarch

1 cup (240 mL) whole milk

3 cups (720 mL) heavy cream

¾ cup (174 g) packed dark brown sugar

Scant ½ teaspoon salt

½ cup (120 mL) water

3 tablespoons unsalted butter

1½ tablespoons scotch, rum, or bourbon

FOR THE CARAMEL SAUCE

½ cup (100 g) granulated sugar

1 tablespoon light corn syrup

1 tablespoon water

⅛ teaspoon fresh lemon juice

⅓ cup (80 mL) heavy cream

½ tablespoon unsalted butter

Generous pinch of salt

FOR SERVING

1 cup (240 mL) heavy cream, cold

Flaky sea salt

HEADS UP

The pudding needs at least 6 hours to chill.

MAKE-AHEAD INSTRUCTIONS

The caramel can be made up to 1 week before serving; the pudding can be refrigerated for up to 2 days before serving; and the whipped cream can be made a few hours ahead of serving.

PRO TIPS

A candy thermometer is not required here, but it takes out any guesswork. There are several different styles of candy thermometers. I prefer the clip-on rectangular models with the thermometer encased in the frame. With this design, the thermometer bulb will not touch the bottom of the pan, even if you rest the thermometer in the pan.

Sugar cooked to high temperatures can cause serious burns. I recommend wearing oven mitts and a long-sleeved shirt (and never test the mixture with your fingers!).

1. Make the pudding: In a medium bowl, combine the egg yolks, cornstarch, and ¼ cup (60 mL) of the milk; whisk until smooth.

2. In a large liquid measuring cup or pitcher, combine the cream and remaining ¾ cup (180 mL) milk.

3. In a 3-quart (3 L) heavy-bottomed pot, stir together the brown sugar, salt, and water; set the pot over high heat. As soon as the mixture starts to boil vigorously around the edges, reduce the heat to medium and cook, without stirring, until darker brown, thickened, foamy, and just starting to smell caramelized (a bit burnt), 9 to 11 minutes. The sugar will bubble vigorously the

-RECIPE CONTINUES-

whole time. If you have a candy thermometer, the butterscotch is ready when it registers 265°F (129°C) to 270°F (132°C). (Be careful not to touch it; it is extremely hot.)

4. Immediately, pour the reserved milk-cream mixture slowly into the butterscotch. The mixture will bubble and steam (be careful!) and the butterscotch will harden up. Bring to a boil, whisking occasionally and scraping the edges of the pot to dissolve the hardened butterscotch, then reduce the heat to low. Slowly whisk 3 ladlefuls of the simmering butterscotch mixture into the reserved egg yolk mixture, whisking constantly to combine. (It's important to whisk constantly so the eggs don't scramble.)

5. Slowly pour the tempered egg yolk mixture into the pot, whisking constantly. Cook, continuing to whisk constantly, until large bubbles burst through the top and the mixture is thickened, about 30 seconds. Turn off the heat and whisk in the butter and scotch.

6. Pour the pudding through a fine-mesh sieve set over a medium bowl, using the back of a ladle or a rubber spatula to push it through (this will remove any bits of cooked egg). Pour the pudding into a large, shallow bowl. Press a piece of plastic wrap onto the surface (to prevent a film from forming) and refrigerate until chilled, at least 6 hours or overnight.

7. Make the caramel sauce: Stir the granulated sugar, corn syrup, water, and lemon juice together in a microwave-safe 2-cup (480 mL) measuring cup or a medium glass bowl. The mixture will be very thick. Microwave until the mixture is pale yellow, or just barely starting to take on some color, 2 to 3 minutes, depending on the strength of your microwave. It's fine to stop and open the microwave to check often; just don't let the caramel get too dark or it will burn. Let the caramel sit on the countertop for 1 to 2 minutes, until it turns a medium honey color.

8. Once the caramel reaches the correct color, slowly pour in the cream, 1 tablespoon at a time, stirring with a soup spoon as you go. The mixture will bubble up intensely, but it shouldn't overflow as long as you add the cream gradually. Once all the cream is added, stir until completely smooth, scraping the bottom and sides of the measuring cup as necessary. Add the butter and salt and stir until the butter is melted. The sauce will seem a bit thin; that's okay, it will thicken up as it cools. Set the caramel aside to cool (you can refrigerate it, covered, for up to a week).

9. Make the whipped cream and serve: In the bowl of an electric mixer fitted with the whisk attachment or beaters, whip the cream on medium speed until soft peaks form. (The whipped cream can be covered with plastic wrap and refrigerated for up to 3 hours.) When ready to serve, whisk the pudding until smooth and spoon evenly into serving bowls. Top the pudding with caramel sauce, whipped cream, and a pinch of flaky sea salt.

Sour Cream Chocolate Loaf Cake

FREEZER-FRIENDLY INSTRUCTIONS

The cake can be frozen, without the glaze, for up to 3 months. Let the cake cool completely, then double-wrap it tightly with aluminum foil or freezer wrap and place in a resealable freezer bag. Thaw overnight in the refrigerator before glazing and serving.

SOURCING SAVVY

The espresso powder enhances the chocolate flavor without adding any discernible coffee taste. If you don't have espresso powder, you can omit it and replace the boiling water with boiling strong coffee.

PRO TIP

A parchment sling is a simple way to get baked goods out of pans without sticking. To make a sling, cut a piece of parchment paper to fit the width of your pan and extend 1 to 2 inches over the sides. These overhanging edges will serve as tabs to easily lift the cake out of the pan once it cools.

Flecked with chocolate chunks and drizzled with a rich, glossy chocolate glaze, this is a lovely cake to have on hand on the weekend for houseguests, and it 100 percent fits the bill when you "just need something chocolate." Because there is melted chocolate in the cake and the glaze, rather than just cocoa powder, it has a fudginess that most chocolate loaf cakes lack, and the addition of sour cream keeps it moist for days.

Serves 8 to 10 (one 9 x 5-inch/23 x 13 cm loaf cake)

FOR THE CAKE

Nonstick cooking spray

4 ounces (114 g) bittersweet chocolate

1½ teaspoons espresso powder or instant espresso (see Sourcing Savvy)

½ cup (120 mL) boiling water

1¾ cups (228 g) all-purpose flour

1½ tablespoons natural unsweetened cocoa powder, such as Hershey's, passed through a fine-mesh sieve to remove lumps

½ teaspoon baking powder

½ teaspoon baking soda

Heaping ½ teaspoon salt

½ cup (1 stick/4 ounces/113 g) unsalted butter, at room temperature

1½ cups (324 g) packed light brown sugar

1½ teaspoons vanilla extract

2 large eggs

½ cup (120 g) sour cream

FOR THE GLAZE

2 tablespoons unsalted butter

1 ounce unsweetened chocolate, coarsely chopped

¾ cup (87 g) confectioners' sugar

2 tablespoons hot water

1. Make the cake: Preheat the oven to 325°F (165°C) and set an oven rack in the middle position. Spray a 9 x 5-inch (23 x 13 cm) loaf pan lightly with nonstick cooking spray. Line the long side of the pan with a parchment paper "sling" (see Pro Tip) and spray lightly again with nonstick cooking spray.

2. Break 1½ ounces (43 g) of the bittersweet chocolate into small pieces and place in a small heatproof bowl. Add the espresso powder. Pour the boiling water over the top and let sit for a few minutes. Stir until the chocolate is melted and the mixture is smooth.

3. Chop the remaining 2½ ounces (71 g) of chocolate into small pieces, no larger than chocolate chips. (The pieces will not be uniform—some will be chunks and some will be shavings—and that's okay.)

4. In a medium bowl, whisk together the flour, cocoa powder, baking powder, baking soda, and salt.

5. In the bowl of an electric mixer fitted with the paddle attachment or beaters, beat the butter, brown sugar, vanilla, and eggs on medium-high speed (or high speed if using a handheld mixer) until smooth, about 1 minute. Add the dry ingredients and mix on low speed, scraping down the sides of the bowl as necessary, until just combined. Add the melted chocolate mixture and the sour cream and mix on low speed until the batter is uniform. Add the chopped chocolate and mix with a rubber spatula, scraping down the sides and bottom of the bowl, until evenly combined.

6. Spoon the batter evenly into the prepared pan. Bake for 55 to 65 minutes, until the cake is set and a toothpick inserted into the center comes out clean. Let the cake cool in the pan for about 15 minutes, then use the parchment sling to lift the cake out onto a rack to cool completely.

7. Make the glaze: Melt the butter in a small saucepan over low heat. Remove the pan from the heat. Add the unsweetened chocolate and whisk until melted. Add the confectioners' sugar and hot water and whisk until completely smooth. If the glaze is too thin, add a bit more confectioners' sugar; if it is too thick, add a touch more water.

8. Place the cooled cake on a serving platter. Using a small spoon, drizzle the glaze over the cake, letting it drip down the sides. Set aside for about 30 minutes to allow the glaze to set. To serve, slice the cake with a serrated knife. (The cake keeps well for up to 4 days, under a cake dome or in a covered container at room temperature.)

Blueberry Cobbler

I love rustic fruit desserts, and this blueberry cobbler with a lemon-scented buttermilk biscuit crust is one of my summertime favorites. As the dessert bakes, the fruit bubbles up into the topping, creating three delicious layers: a tart, syrupy blueberry bottom, a dumpling-like center, and a crisp, golden crust. One key to a delicious cobbler is getting the right ratio of fruit to crust. This topping is generous and lends just the right amount of savory buttery flavor to balance the tart-sweetness of the berries.

Serves 6 to 8

FOR THE FRUIT FILLING

2 tablespoons unsalted butter, cut into small pieces, plus more for greasing the pan

4 cups (560 g) fresh blueberries

¾ cup (150 g) sugar

2 tablespoons all-purpose flour

FOR THE BISCUIT TOPPING

1½ cups (195 g) all-purpose flour

7 tablespoons (88 g) sugar

1 teaspoon packed grated lemon zest (from 1 lemon)

1¾ teaspoons baking powder

¼ teaspoon baking soda

¾ teaspoon salt

½ cup (1 stick/4 ounces/113 g) cold unsalted butter, cut into small chunks

1 cup (240 mL) buttermilk

Vanilla ice cream or Sweetened Whipped Cream (see sidebar), for serving

PRO TIP

When baking with berries, there's always some variation in the sweetness of the fruit. Taste the blueberries; if they happen to be very sweet, reduce the sugar in the filling to ⅔ cup (133 g).

SWEETENED WHIPPED CREAM

In the bowl of a stand mixer fitted with the whisk attachment (or in a large bowl if using a hand mixer) beat 1 cup (240 mL) of cold heavy cream until it starts to thicken. Add 2 tablespoons confectioners' sugar and beat until soft to medium peaks form.

1. Preheat the oven to 375°F (190°C) and set an oven rack in the middle position. Grease an 8-inch (20 cm) square or 2-quart (2 L) baking dish with butter.

2. Make the fruit filling: In a large bowl, toss the blueberries with the sugar and flour. Transfer the mixture to the prepared baking dish and dot evenly with the 2 tablespoons of butter.

3. Make the biscuit topping: In a medium bowl, combine the flour, 6 tablespoons of the sugar, and the lemon zest, baking powder, baking soda, and salt. Add the butter and blend with your fingers or a pastry cutter until the mixture resembles coarse crumbs with pea-sized clumps of butter within. Add the buttermilk and stir with a spoon until just combined. It will look a bit lumpy; that's good. Do not overmix.

4. Using a large spoon, dollop 8 to 10 spoonfuls of the batter over the blueberries, allowing the filling to peek through in spots (most of the filling will be covered). Sprinkle the remaining tablespoon sugar over the batter.

5. Bake until the fruit is bubbling and the biscuit top is golden, about 35 minutes. Cover loosely with foil and bake for 10 minutes more. Remove the foil and let cool for 15 to 20 minutes. Serve with vanilla ice cream or the whipped cream.

Peanut Butter & Jam Thumbprints

HEADS UP

The cookie dough needs at least 1 hour to chill before baking.

MAKE-AHEAD/FREEZER-FRIENDLY INSTRUCTIONS

The dough can be made and refrigerated up to 1 day ahead of time. The baked cookies can be frozen for up to 3 months. To freeze, let the cookies cool completely, then freeze them on the baking sheet until set before transferring them to an airtight container. Before serving, remove the cookies from the container and let them come to room temperature.

PRO TIP

In baking, sometimes the brands you use can make all the difference, especially in cookie recipes. I use King Arthur all-purpose flour, which is higher in protein than many other brands. In recipe testing, I found that these cookies turned out much prettier (and rounder) using King Arthur flour compared to other brands.

These old-fashioned peanut butter thumbprint cookies are made by rolling peanut butter cookie dough into balls, indenting them with the back of a wooden spoon (or your thumb, hence the name), and filling them with a dollop of glistening blackberry jam (strawberry, raspberry, or mixed berry jams work, too, but blackberry is my favorite). Like PB&J in dessert form, they are salty, sweet, soft, and rich . . . not to mention cute as can be!

Makes 3 dozen

1½ cups (195 g) all-purpose flour

½ teaspoon baking powder

½ teaspoon baking soda

½ teaspoon salt

½ cup (1 stick/4 ounces/113 g) unsalted butter, at room temperature

1 cup (260 g) creamy peanut butter, such as Skippy, at room temperature (do not use natural peanut butter)

¾ cup (174 g) packed dark brown sugar

¼ cup (50 g) granulated sugar, plus more for rolling

1 teaspoon vanilla extract

1 large egg

About ½ cup (160 g) blackberry jam, jelly, or preserves

1. In a medium bowl, whisk together the flour, baking powder, baking soda, and salt.

2. In the bowl of an electric mixer fitted with the paddle attachment or beaters, beat the butter, peanut butter, brown sugar, granulated sugar, and vanilla on medium speed until well combined, about 1 minute. Scrape down the sides of the bowl with a rubber spatula. Add the egg and beat on medium speed until incorporated, about 20 seconds more. Add the dry ingredients and mix on low speed until just combined, scraping the sides of the bowl as necessary. Refrigerate the dough for 1 hour, or until firm enough to roll.

3. Preheat the oven to 350°F (175°C) and set an oven rack in the middle position. Line a 13 x 18-inch (33 x 46 cm) baking sheet with parchment paper.

4. Roll the dough into very smooth tablespoon-size balls (making them smooth and seamless will help avoid cracks when the cookies bake), then roll in a bowl of granulated sugar and place 2 inches (5 cm) apart on the prepared baking sheet. Using the rounded end of a wooden spoon, make an indentation in the center of each cookie, pressing about three-fourths of the way down. Bake until puffed and set, about 8 minutes.

5. Meanwhile, place the jam in a small microwave-safe bowl. Microwave on high until slightly runny but not liquid, 15 to 20 seconds. (Alternatively, heat the jam on the stovetop.)

6. Remove the baking sheet from the oven and, using a very small spoon, fill the center of each cookie with jam. Return the cookies to the oven and bake for 3 minutes more. Let the cookies cool on the baking sheet for a few minutes, then transfer them to a wire rack to cool completely. (Store the cookies in a single layer in an airtight container for up to 3 days.)

Rustic Plum Tart

Whether you call it a rustic plum tart (American), a plum galette (French), or a plum crostata (Italian), you're going to love this gorgeous summer dessert. With a crackly pastry crust folded over a filling of finely chopped almonds and luscious purple plums, it's essentially a free-form pie baked on a sheet pan, and it has a deliciously high crust-to-fruit ratio. The purpose of the almonds is twofold: they add wonderful flavor and help absorb some of the plum juices so the crust doesn't get soggy.

If you're intimidated by making your own crust, don't be! My all-butter tart crust is not only easy to make but also very forgiving, and it comes together in less than one minute in a food processor. It makes a fabulous base for any fruit tart. Although, if you have crust-lovers in your house like I do, beware of late-night snackers who steal the pleated crust and leave you with only the center of the tart.

Serves 8

FOR THE FILLING AND GLAZE

½ cup (50 g) sliced almonds

2 tablespoons all-purpose flour

¼ cup plus ⅓ cup (117 g) granulated sugar

1 pound (454 g) fresh red or black plums (3 or 4), pitted and sliced ¼ inch (6 mm) thick

1 large egg, beaten

1 tablespoon turbinado or coarse sugar

2 tablespoons apricot jam (best quality)

FOR THE CRUST

1½ cups (195 g) all-purpose flour

½ teaspoon salt

2 tablespoons granulated sugar

¾ cup (1½ sticks/6 ounces/170 g) very cold unsalted butter, cut into ½-inch (13 mm) pieces

¼ cup (60 mL) very cold water

MAKE-AHEAD/FREEZER-FRIENDLY INSTRUCTIONS

The dough can be made up to 3 days in advance and refrigerated. Allow it to sit at room temperature for about 15 minutes, or until pliable, before rolling. The assembled tart may be frozen for up to 3 months. To freeze, place the baking sheet in the freezer until the tart is frozen, then wrap the tart tightly. Bake directly from the freezer, adding a few extra minutes to the baking time.

PRO TIP

I know it can be tempting to load up the tart with extra plums, but less is more here. Stone fruits give off a ton of juice, which can leak from the tart and make a mess of the crust and your pan.

1. Line a 13 x 18-inch (33 x 46 cm) sheet pan with parchment paper.

2. Start the filling: In the bowl of a food processor, process the almonds until finely chopped, about 1 minute. Transfer to a small bowl.

3. Make the crust: To the bowl of the food processor (no need to clean it), add the flour, salt, and granulated sugar; pulse briefly to combine. Add the butter and process just until the butter is the size of peas, about 5 seconds. Sprinkle the water over the mixture and process until just moistened and very crumbly, about 5 seconds.

4. Transfer the dough to a lightly floured work surface and knead it a few times, just until it comes together into a cohesive ball. Pat the dough into

-RECIPE CONTINUES-

a disk. Flour your work surface again and dust the dough with flour. Using a rolling pin, roll the dough into a circle 8 to 10 inches (20 to 25 cm) in diameter, turning it and adding more flour as necessary to avoid sticking. Transfer the dough to the prepared baking sheet and refrigerate for 15 minutes. (You'll roll the dough out further, directly on the parchment, so go ahead and clean your work surface.)

5. Take the dough out of the fridge and slide the parchment onto the countertop. Directly on the parchment, roll the dough into a 13-inch (33 cm) circle about ⅛ inch (3 mm) thick. It's fine if the edges are a little ragged. Slide the parchment and dough back onto the baking sheet—the dough will run up the lip of the sheet pan slightly.

6. Complete the filling: Sprinkle the 2 tablespoons of flour evenly over the pastry, leaving a 1-inch (2.5 cm) border. Sprinkle the chopped almonds evenly over the flour, followed by ¼ cup (50 g) of the granulated sugar. Arrange the plum slices on top in overlapping concentric circles to within about 2½ inches (6 cm) of the edge. Don't worry about making it look perfect; it doesn't make much difference in the end, and you don't want the dough to get too warm. Sprinkle the remaining ⅓ cup (67 g) granulated sugar over the plums.

7. Fold the edges of the dough over the plums in a free-form fashion, working your way around and creating pleats as you go. Patch up any tears by pinching a bit of dough from the edge.

8. Using a pastry brush, brush the pleated dough evenly with the beaten egg. Sprinkle the turbinado sugar over the crust. Chill the assembled tart in the refrigerator for 15 to 20 minutes.

9. Meanwhile, preheat the oven to 350°F (175°C) and set an oven rack in the middle position.

10. Bake the tart for 55 to 65 minutes, or until the plums are tender and the crust is golden brown. (It's okay if some of the juices leak from the tart onto the pan. The juices will burn on the pan but the tart should be fine—just scrape any burnt bits away from the crust once it's baked.) Transfer the tart to a rack and let cool.

11. While the tart cools, make the glaze. Microwave the apricot jam in a small, microwave-safe bowl until bubbling, 10 to 20 seconds. Using a pastry brush, brush the plums with the jam until glistening.

12. Use 2 large spatulas to transfer the tart to a serving plate or cutting board. Slice and serve warm or at room temperature. The tart is best served the day it is made, but leftovers will keep nicely, loosely covered on the countertop, for a few days.

Kentucky Bourbon Cake

The foundation for this drunken pound cake is the famous Kentucky butter cake, which has been around since at least 1963, when Nell Lewis of Platte City, Missouri, entered it into the Pillsbury Bake-Off contest and won. Her original recipe is an old-fashioned vanilla buttermilk pound cake drenched in a luscious butter and sugar syrup. The syrup not only moistens the cake—and I mean *really* moistens—but also creates a crisp coating on the surface, almost like a glazed donut. I've tweaked her recipe and swapped out some of the liquid in the cake and glaze with bourbon. As you can imagine, a boozy butter cake like this is hard to resist. Thank you to my longtime reader Karen Tannenbaum for sharing the Kentucky butter cake recipe with me!

Makes one 10-inch Bundt cake

FOR THE CAKE

Nonstick cooking spray with flour, such as Baker's Joy or Pam Baking

¾ cup (180 mL) buttermilk

¼ cup (60 ml) bourbon

4 large eggs

2 teaspoons vanilla extract

3 cups (390 g) all-purpose flour

2 cups (400 g) granulated sugar

1 teaspoon baking powder

½ teaspoon baking soda

1 teaspoon salt

1 cup (2 sticks/8 ounces/226 g) unsalted butter, at room temperature

Confectioners' sugar, for dusting (optional)

FOR THE GLAZE

6 tablespoons (¾ stick/3 ounces/85 g) unsalted butter

¾ cup (150 g) granulated sugar

¼ cup (60 mL) bourbon

1½ tablespoons water

Pinch of salt

1. Make the cake: Preheat the oven to 325°F (165°C) and set an oven rack in the middle position. Spray a 10-inch/12-cup (2.8 L) Bundt pan with nonstick cooking spray with flour.

2. In a medium bowl, whisk together the buttermilk, bourbon, eggs, and vanilla. (Note that the mixture will start to look curdled as it sits—that's okay.)

3. In the bowl of an electric mixer fitted with the paddle attachment or beaters, combine the flour, granulated sugar, baking powder, baking soda, and salt. Beat on low speed for 30 seconds to combine. Add the butter and half the buttermilk mixture and mix on low speed until moistened but still a little crumbly, about 1 minute. With the mixer on low, gradually add the remaining buttermilk mixture, then increase the speed to medium and mix for 3 minutes,

-RECIPE CONTINUES-

FREEZER-FRIENDLY INSTRUCTIONS

Once the glaze on the cake is completely set, the cake can be wrapped tightly in plastic freezer wrap and frozen for up to 3 months. Before serving, let the cake thaw on the countertop overnight.

PRO TIP

This is a high-ratio cake, which means that the weight of the sugar equals or exceeds the weight of the flour. Why does this matter? Instead of the more common "creaming" method, in which the butter and sugar are beaten together before the eggs, flour, and liquid are added, high-ratio cakes can be made using the "high-ratio" or "quick-mix" method. This involves mixing all the dry ingredients with the butter and some of the liquid first, then adding the remaining liquid ingredients. This method is not only faster and easier than the traditional creaming method but also yields incredibly tender and fine-textured cakes.

stopping once to scrape down the sides and bottom of the bowl with a rubber spatula. The batter should look pale and creamy. Scrape down the sides and bottom of the bowl again, making sure the batter is evenly mixed.

4. Transfer the batter to the prepared pan and bake for about 1 hour, until a cake tester comes out clean.

5. Make the glaze: Meanwhile, melt the butter in a small saucepan over medium heat. Add the granulated sugar, bourbon, water, and salt. Bring to a gentle boil, then reduce the heat and simmer, whisking constantly, until the sugar is dissolved, about 1 minute.

6. Set the baked cake, still in the pan, on a cooling rack. Using a skewer or toothpick, poke about 40 holes in the bottom of the warm cake, going about three-fourths of the way down. Spoon half the glaze evenly over the bottom of the cake. If the glaze starts to pool on the surface, poke more holes to help it sink in. Leave the cake on the rack for 30 minutes.

7. Invert the cake onto a serving platter. Brush the remaining glaze evenly over the top and sides of the cake, letting it set as you go and adding additional coats until you run out. Let the cake sit for at least 1 hour before serving. Using a fine-mesh sieve, dust the cake with confectioners' sugar, if desired. The cake will keep nicely for 2 to 3 days, stored in a cake dome at room temperature.

Triple Chocolate Cheesecake

After making my go-to New York cheesecake for years for family celebrations, my son, Zach, a chocolate lover after my own heart, suggested we add a chocolate version to the mix. I tried many recipes but always found the flavor to be a bit off. While the tanginess of cream cheese works beautifully with vanilla, lemon, and fruit flavors, it doesn't always complement chocolate. Finally, I realized that the secret to a really good chocolate cheesecake is to use mild milk chocolate. Rich, dense, and decadent, this milk chocolate cheesecake with an Oreo crust and chocolate ganache topping is now my most requested.

Serves 12 to 14

FOR THE COOKIE CRUST

Nonstick cooking spray

1 (10-ounce/286 g) package Oreo Thins (2 cups/286 g crumbs)

¼ cup (50 g) sugar

3 tablespoons unsalted butter, at room temperature

FOR THE CHOCOLATE CHEESECAKE FILLING

8 ounces (227 g) milk chocolate, finely chopped

4 (8-ounce/226 g) packages cream cheese, at room temperature

1½ cups (300 g) sugar

¼ cup (20 g) natural unsweetened cocoa powder, such as Hershey's

1 tablespoon vanilla extract

¼ teaspoon salt

4 large eggs

FOR THE CHOCOLATE GANACHE TOPPING

½ cup (120 mL) heavy cream

2 tablespoons light corn syrup

4 ounces (113 g) semisweet chocolate, finely chopped

HEADS UP

You will need 18-inch (457 mm) heavy-duty aluminum foil for this recipe (see Pro Tip). The cheesecake needs to chill for at least 8 hours, and the ganache needs to set on the cheesecake for 1 hour, before serving.

MAKE-AHEAD/FREEZER-FRIENDLY INSTRUCTIONS

The cheesecake can be made and stored in the springform pan in the refrigerator, tightly covered with plastic wrap, up to two days ahead of time. The cheesecake can also be frozen (without the chocolate ganache topping) for up to 3 months. To freeze, place the cake, unwrapped, in the freezer briefly to firm it up. Then double-wrap it tightly with aluminum foil or plastic freezer wrap and place it in a resealable freezer bag. Thaw in the refrigerator overnight before you plan to serve it. Add the ganache topping at least 1 hour before serving, so it has time to set.

1. Make the cookie crust: Preheat the oven to 375°F (190°C) and set an oven rack in the lower-middle position. Wrap the outside of a 9- or 10-inch (23 or 25 cm) springform pan with a large piece of heavy-duty aluminum foil, covering the underside and extending all the way to the top so there are no seams on the bottom or sides of the pan. For insurance, repeat with a second sheet of foil. Spray the inside of the pan with nonstick cooking spray.

2. In a food processor, process the cookies until finely ground. Add the sugar and butter and process until well blended. Press the crumbs evenly into the bottom of the prepared pan. Bake until just set, about 10 minutes. Remove the pan from the oven and set aside to cool while preparing the filling. Reduce the oven temperature to 325°F (165°C).

3. Make the chocolate cheesecake filling: Set a full kettle of water to boil (you'll use this to create the water bath to bake the cheesecake in step 5). Place the chopped milk chocolate in a medium microwave-safe glass bowl.

-RECIPE CONTINUES-

Springform pans are notorious for leaking. Since the cheesecake bakes in a water bath, the aluminum foil prevents the water from seeping in during baking. Please do not attempt to use standard 12-inch (30 cm) aluminum foil—you must not have any foil seams on the bottom or sides of the pan. I can tell you from experience that no matter how well (or how many times) you wrap the pan, the water will find a way in if there are seams in the foil. Even when wrapped properly, you can occasionally get some condensation inside the foil. If this happens, don't worry—the crust is likely just a bit moist around the edges. Simply remove the sides of the springform pan before refrigerating and let the crust dry out in the refrigerator.

The water bath (also called a *bain-marie*) regulates the temperature and keeps the cheesecake baking at an even, low heat. The steam created by the water bath also protects the cheesecake from drying out and cracking.

Microwave in two to three 30-second intervals, stirring in between, until the chocolate is mostly melted and just a few small pieces remain. Stir, allowing the residual heat in the bowl to melt the remaining chocolate pieces. (Alternatively, place the chopped chocolate in a metal bowl set over a saucepan of simmering water and stir until melted and smooth.) Set aside to cool slightly.

4. In the bowl of an electric mixer fitted with the paddle attachment or beaters, beat the cream cheese, sugar, cocoa powder, vanilla, and salt on medium speed until smooth, scraping down the sides of the bowl as necessary. Add the eggs one at a time, beating on medium-low speed until smooth after each addition. Mix in the melted milk chocolate, scraping down the sides of the bowl as necessary. Make sure the mixture is uniform, but do not overmix.

5. Check to make sure the oven has cooled to 325°F (165°C), then set the springform pan in a large roasting pan. Pour the filling over the crust. Pour boiling water into the large roasting pan until it reaches about 1 inch (2.5 cm) up the sides of the cake pan. Bake until the cheesecake is just set, about 1 hour 30 minutes to 1 hour 45 minutes. (The cake should not look at all liquidy, but will wobble just a bit when the pan is nudged; it will continue to cook as it cools.) Carefully remove the roasting pan from the oven and set it on a wire rack. Cool the cheesecake in the water bath until the water is just warm, about 45 minutes.

6. Remove the springform pan from the water bath and discard the foil. If necessary, run a thin-bladed knife around the edge of the cheesecake to make sure it's not sticking to the sides (which can cause cracks as it cools), then cover with plastic wrap and transfer to the refrigerator to cool for at least 8 hours or overnight (leave the sides of the springform pan on).

7. Make the chocolate ganache topping: Pour the cream and corn syrup into a microwave-safe medium bowl. Microwave on high until boiling, about 1 minute. Add the chopped semisweet chocolate. (Alternatively, place the chocolate in a medium bowl. In a small saucepan, bring the cream and corn syrup to a boil and then pour it over the chocolate.) Let the mixture sit for 30 seconds, then whisk until the chocolate melts and the mixture is smooth and glossy. Let the ganache cool until slightly thickened but still pourable, whisking occasionally so a film doesn't form on top, about 30 minutes. (If it gets too thick, you can warm it in the microwave in 10-second intervals, stirring in between, until just pourable.)

8. Remove the sides of the springform pan and place the cheesecake on a serving platter. (You don't have to remove the base of the pan, but if you would like to, run a long, thin spatula between the crust and the pan bottom, then use 2 large spatulas to carefully transfer the cheesecake to the serving platter.)

9. Pour the cooled ganache over the center of cheesecake, and spread it with an offset spatula to the edges, letting it drip a bit down the sides (you may not need all of it). Chill until the topping is set, about 1 hour. Slice the cheesecake with a sharp knife, wiping the knife clean between slices.

Gingerbread Cupcakes
WITH CREAM CHEESE FROSTING

If you like ginger cookies and gingerbread, you'll love these spiced cupcakes—especially how they fill your home with the scent of the holidays as they bake in the oven. I adorn the tops with slivers of crystallized ginger, which deepen their lovely ginger flavor and add a little zip, but you could also dress them up with festive sugar pearls or sparkling sugar.

Serves 12

FOR THE CUPCAKES

1½ cups (195 g) all-purpose flour

1 teaspoon baking powder

¼ teaspoon baking soda

½ teaspoon salt

2 teaspoons ground ginger

1 teaspoon ground cinnamon

½ teaspoon ground cloves

⅛ teaspoon freshly ground black pepper

½ cup (1 stick/4 ounces/113 g) unsalted butter, at room temperature

¼ cup (50 g) granulated sugar

¼ cup (54 g) packed light brown sugar

1 large egg

½ cup (120 mL) unsulphured molasses, preferably Grandma's

½ cup (120 mL) milk

FOR THE FROSTING

6 ounces (170 g) cream cheese, at room temperature

6 tablespoons (¾ stick/3 ounces/ 85 g) unsalted butter, at room temperature

½ teaspoon vanilla extract

Pinch of salt

3 cups (348 g) confectioners' sugar

Crystallized ginger, for topping (optional)

FREEZER-FRIENDLY INSTRUCTIONS

The unfrosted cupcakes can be frozen for up to 3 months. Let them first cool completely before wrapping individually in plastic and then in foil. Thaw overnight on the countertop before frosting and serving.

SOURCING SAVVY

Crystallized ginger, which is fresh ginger root that has been cooked in a simple syrup, dried, and rolled in coarse sugar, has a sweet-spicy flavor and a slightly chewy texture. I find it in the spice aisle of my supermarket; if you don't see it there, it may be near the dried fruit and nuts or the baking ingredients.

PRO TIP

I suggest using a handheld electric mixer for this recipe rather than a stand mixer. (There isn't a lot of batter, so with a stand mixer, you will have to constantly scrape the sides of the bowl.)

1. Make the cupcakes: Preheat the oven to 350°F (175°C) and set an oven rack in the middle position. Line a 12-cup muffin pan with paper liners.

2. In a medium bowl, whisk together the flour, baking powder, baking soda, salt, ginger, cinnamon, cloves, and black pepper.

3. In the bowl of an electric mixer fitted with the beaters or the paddle attachment, cream the butter, granulated sugar, and brown sugar on medium speed until light and fluffy, about 2 minutes. Beat in the egg, then add the molasses and beat until smooth, about 30 seconds.

4. With the mixer on low speed, beat in one-third of the flour mixture, followed by half the milk. (The batter will curdle; that's okay.) Scrape down the sides of the bowl. Add another third of the flour mixture, followed by the remaining milk, and then the remaining flour mixture. Scrape down the bowl and beat again until the batter is just combined. The mixture may look a bit grainy or curdled; again, that's okay.

-RECIPE CONTINUES-

5. Spoon the batter into the prepared muffin pan, filling each cup about three-fourths full. Bake for 20 to 22 minutes, until the cupcakes are set and a toothpick or cake tester inserted into the center of a cupcake comes out clean. Let cool in the pan for about 10 minutes, then transfer to a wire rack to cool completely. The cupcakes will be flat; that's okay.

6. Make the frosting: In the bowl of an electric mixer fitted with the beaters or the paddle attachment, beat the cream cheese, butter, vanilla, and salt on low speed until combined. Increase the speed to medium high and beat until aerated and light, about 2 minutes. Gradually add the confectioners' sugar, mixing on low to combine. Once all of the sugar is mixed in, increase the speed to medium high and beat until fluffy, about 1 minute.

7. When the cupcakes are completely cooled, use a butter knife or small offset spatula to swirl the frosting lavishly over the top. Sprinkle a few pieces of crystallized ginger on the center of each cupcake if desired. (Store the cupcakes in a covered container for up to 1 day.)

Sweet Potato Praline Pie

A marriage of sweet potato pie and pecan pie, with a generous splash of bourbon, this is a standout holiday dessert. The inspiration comes from the *Red Truck Bakery Cookbook*, a charming collection of nostalgic yet elevated recipes from the beloved bakery in rural Virginia. They refer to their original version as "The Presidential Pie" because President Barack Obama made it famous by sharing a photo of himself eating a slice, with the caption, "I like pie. That's not a state secret. And I can confirm that the Red Truck Bakery makes some darn good pie." You don't have to make your own crust, but if you have the time, it really does take this pie to the next level.

Serves 8 (Makes one 9-inch/23 cm deep-dish pie)

1 (9-inch/23 cm) deep-dish Homemade Pie Crust (page 281) or frozen pie crust shell (thawed)

FOR THE SWEET POTATO FILLING

1½ cups (370 g) mashed sweet potatoes (from 2 large sweet potatoes; see Pro Tip)

3 tablespoons unsalted butter, melted

¾ cup (162 g) packed light brown sugar

1 large egg

1 large egg yolk

1½ tablespoons bourbon

3 tablespoons heavy cream

Heaping ¼ teaspoon ground cinnamon

Heaping ¼ teaspoon ground nutmeg

¼ teaspoon salt

FOR THE PECAN TOPPING

6 tablespoons (81 g) light brown sugar

1 large egg

6 tablespoons (90 mL) light corn syrup

2 tablespoons unsalted butter, melted

1 tablespoon bourbon

⅛ teaspoon salt

1¼ cups (150 g) chopped pecans

MAKE-AHEAD/FREEZER-FRIENDLY INSTRUCTIONS
The pie can be prepared up to 1 day ahead of time, covered with aluminum foil, and stored at room temperature. The baked pie also freezes well for up to 3 months. Cool the pie completely and wrap it in several layers of plastic wrap, and then a layer of aluminum foil. Thaw the pie overnight in the refrigerator and allow it to come to room temperature before serving.

PRO TIP
To make the mashed sweet potatoes, preheat the oven to 400°F (205°C). Line a baking sheet with aluminum foil. Prick each sweet potato 5 or 6 times with a fork, then place on the prepared baking sheet. Roast until very tender, about 1 hour. Let cool, then scoop out the pulp into a medium bowl. Using a potato masher or fork, mash until smooth.

1. Preheat the oven to 375°F (190°C) and set an oven rack in the middle position.

2. If using the homemade crust, cover the chilled crust with a piece of parchment paper. Fill the crust at least halfway full with dried beans or pie weights. Bake for 17 to 20 minutes, until the crust is pale and partially cooked. Remove the parchment and dried beans or pie weights. Reduce the oven temperature to 325°F (165°C). If using a frozen crust, follow the instructions for blind-baking on the package. After baking, reduce the oven temperature to 325°F/165°C.

-RECIPE CONTINUES-

3. Make the sweet potato filling: In the bowl of an electric mixer fitted with the paddle attachment or beaters, beat the mashed sweet potatoes on medium speed until creamy and smooth, about 1 minute. Add the butter, brown sugar, egg, egg yolk, bourbon, cream, cinnamon, nutmeg, and salt; beat on medium speed, scraping down the sides as necessary, until thoroughly mixed. Pour the sweet potato filling into the parbaked pie shell.

4. Make the pecan topping: In a medium bowl, combine the brown sugar, egg, corn syrup, butter, bourbon, and salt; whisk until thoroughly combined.

5. Pour half the topping mixture (about ½ cup/120 mL) over the sweet potato filling. Scatter the pecans in a single layer over the top. Drizzle the remaining topping mixture over the pecans, making sure they are all coated.

6. Check to make sure the oven temperature has reached 325°F (165°C). Bake for 55 to 65 minutes, or until the filling is set. Transfer the pie to a rack and let cool completely before serving.

Homemade Pie Crust

This is my go-to pie crust recipe. The butter gives the crust a wonderful flavor and flaky texture, while the shortening makes the dough easy to work with and also helps it hold its shape in the oven. Adding a bit of baking powder to the dough helps the crust expand into the pan, rather than shrink and slip down the sides as it bakes (a genius trick I picked up from the pastry chef Nick Malgieri).

PRO TIP

It's important that the butter and shortening both be very cold, so keep them in the refrigerator until you're ready to add them.

Makes one 9-inch (23 cm) deep-dish pie crust

1½ cups (195 g) all-purpose flour

½ teaspoon salt

⅛ teaspoon baking powder

6 tablespoons (¾ stick/3 ounces/ 85 g) cold unsalted butter, sliced into ¼-inch (6 mm) pieces

3 tablespoons cold vegetable shortening, in 3 pieces

4 tablespoons (60 mL) cold water

1. Combine the flour, salt, and baking powder in a food processor fitted with the metal blade. Process for 5 seconds to blend.

2. Add the butter and shortening. Pulse until you have coarse crumbs with lots of pea-sized clumps of butter and shortening within, fifteen to twenty 1-second pulses.

3. Add the water and pulse until the mixture is just evenly moistened and very crumbly, seven to ten 1-second pulses.

4. Turn the crumbly dough out onto a work surface and gather it into a ball.

5. Pat the dough into a 5-inch (13 cm) disk and wrap it in plastic. Refrigerate for at least 45 minutes or up to 3 days to rest.

6. Take the dough out of the refrigerator and dust your work surface lightly with flour. Place the dough on top and sprinkle with a little flour. With your hands, quickly knead the dough into a soft, malleable disk (don't overwork it; you want it just supple enough to roll).

7. Roll out the dough into a 13-inch (33 cm) circle, turning it frequently and adding more flour as necessary to prevent sticking.

8. Gently fold the dough into quarters without creasing it and transfer it to a 9-inch (23 cm) deep-dish pie pan. Gently fit the dough into the pan, easing it in rather than stretching it out. Don't worry if it tears, just patch it right back up.

9. Trim the edges to ½ inch (13 mm) beyond the lip of the pie pan if necessary. Fold the edges under to create a rim on the crust (you can use the scraps to patch in any thin areas), then press the rim against the lip of the pan, forming it into an even edge as you go. Using your fingers, crimp the rim. Place the crust in the refrigerator for at least 30 minutes to firm up, and then proceed with your pie recipe.

Acknowledgements

Writing a cookbook is a labor of love, and I am filled with so much gratitude for everyone who helped bring *Weeknight/Weekend* to life.

To my fearless and brilliant agent, Maria Ribas, thank you for your tireless work on this book, and for taking care of business and matching me with the most amazing team at Clarkson Potter. I am so lucky to have you in my corner.

To my editor, Raquel Pelzel, thank you for your wisdom and guidance, and for believing in this book from the start. It is truly a joy to work with you. To Stephanie Huntwork, Sonia Persad, and Jan Derevjanik for designing such a beautiful and approachable cookbook. And to the rest of the Clarkson Potter team, who shepherded this book from concept to creation: Aaron Wehner, Francis Lam, Stephanie Davis, Windy Davis, Erica Gelbard, Serena Wang, Kelli Tokos, and Bianca Cruz.

To Johnny Miller, who bravely shot the photos for this book mid-pandemic with his kids doing school online in the next room. To Rebecca Jurkevich and Cybelle Tondu, for styling the food and making it look so effortlessly perfect. And to Sarah Smart, for all of the gorgeous props that brought the photos to life.

Thank you to my *Once Upon a Chef* family, especially Betsy Goldstein for being my right-hand person and also a dear friend. You make this work so much more fun. A special thanks to the lovely Lacy Walpert for being part of the team and testing recipes, and Kelly Santoro, my bestie since seventh grade, for testing recipes and converting the recipes to metric.

To Michael, my partner in all things and anchor for over twenty years, and my kids, Zach and Anna—thank you for being my best critics and biggest cheerleaders, and for bringing so much love and laughter into my life. Having you all around the table, with Ollie and Gus underneath it, is the best part of every meal. Thank you to my sister, Erica, for her sharp creative eye and willingness to lend an ear. And Mom and Dad, too, for always encouraging me to chase my dreams, and for showing me how it's done. I love you all.

To my volunteer recipe testers, how can I ever express my gratitude? Your enthusiasm and willingness to test recipes during such challenging times, when it was difficult to even go to the grocery store, was generous beyond measure. Your feedback, emails, and photos were invaluable, and I absolutely loved sharing the process with you.

Finally, to my *Once Upon a Chef* blog readers, thank you for welcoming me into your kitchens, sharing my recipes near and far, and taking this journey with me. I am forever grateful.

Index

Note: Page numbers in *italics* indicate photos.